TACKLING NOTRE DAME

To
Laurie,
my vivacious,
intelligent, pretty
student — —
fourth row,
third from the back,
— best wishes
& love,
always —

Virginia Morrow Black

TACKLING NOTRE DAME

Virginia Morrow Black

HALLBERG
PUBLISHING CORPORATION
ISBN 087319
DELAVAN, WI & WESTPORT, CT

ISBN Number 0-87319-030-0
Library of Congress Catalog Card No. 85-081021
Copyright © Virginia Morrow Black. All rights reserved.
Manufactured in the U.S.A. First printing August 1985.
No part of this book may be reproduced without permission
from HALLBERG PUBLISHING CORPORATION.

Direct all inquiries to:
HALLBERG PUBLISHING CORPORATION
P.O. Box 547
Delavan, Wisconsin 53115

Contents

Foreword
Bernard Norling

The pursuit of higher education is long, and especially for the newly wedded, expensive. Many a young wife has emulated the author of this book: e.g. racked her brain to devise some way to augment the family income while her husband went to school. Many other women have doggedly pursued literary ambitions. Some have taken the plunge into politics. But few have combined these and kindred endeavors with such a combination of zeal and unorthodoxy as Virginia Black.

For years Mrs. Black wrote poems, plays, essays and books, but her main publications were Letters to the Editor of the local newspaper. Her friends introduced her, teasingly, as "America's leading unpublished author;" and indeed, for a long time her biggest payday as a writer came on an occasion when she was reimbursed for something that was not published.

Twice Virginia strove to make a career as a professional contestant: a composer of 25-word responses to such enigmatic declarations as "I feed my housecat Rocky Mountain Pickled Herring because . . . ." At various times she won such prizes as a sewing machine (when she had not yet learned how to sew), a $400 electric car for small children when the family could hardly scrape together $33 for a month's rent, ten cans of food with the labels removed, a dog, a pair of roller skates, a subscription to a comic magazine and most appropriately, an empty billfold.

She took a job in a department store. Her first task was to look for a lost parakeet. Her mercantile career ended soon after when she sold a customer two left shoes. She tried teaching second graders in a school whose inmates contemplated civilization but declined to embrace it. After a year she resolved never to teach again. Years later she strove to become a professional angle-worm producer, but a savage northern Indiana winter froze out her stock.

The political career of Virginia Black was comparably abortive. For sixteen years her Congressional district was served by a statesman who regularly rolled up such huge majorities at the polls that at length no sacrificial lamb from the opposing party could be induced to stand against him. Piqued, Virginia decided one evening, while stirring spaghetti sauce, to run for Congress. It was symbolic of her campaign that she began it by asking this writer to be her campaign manager. I have such a lifelong affinity for lost causes that had I been in London in 1912 I surely would have bought a ticket on the TITANIC. I proved to be sadly typical of Virginia's aides. One key member of her "brains trust" invariably brought a half gallon jug of wine to "strategy" conferences. Two Party functionaries who were supposed to lend their professional expertise to the campaign were so incompatible that they got into a fist fight at that highlight of the Indiana social season, a corn roast. Not surprisingly, the incumbent won the election with his customary ease.

A born loser, one might conclude, a most unlikely person to help a husband negotiate anything, much less graduate school at a major university. But appearances are proverbially deceiving. Luck in life, as in cards, evens out, and those who persevere grow luckier. Virginia's husband eventually became Dr. Anthony Black, for many years now a Professor of History at St. Mary's College. Virginia herself, is now a published writer; and the tyro who once despaired after daily confrontations with barbarous seven-year-olds got her second wind and lived on to be voted favorite Teacher in a nearby high school.

Preface

Ever since World War II the married student on college campuses across the United States became an integral part of academia. The seeking of advanced degrees by many of the returning veterans, supplemented by the G.I. Bill, caused a virtual flood in applications for the Doctor of Philosophy degree — the Ph.D., in various disciplines. Little has been written, however, about the correlative degree that the married student's partner simultaneously receives upon the Ph.D.'s graduation, — the Ph.T., which simply stands for: Putting him or her Through.

TACKLING NOTRE DAME is a nostalgic testimonial of the earnings of two such degrees. It is a fun chronicle about life the way it was at the University of Notre Dame's Vetville in the 1950's. Vetville was the married students' community that was comprised of 114 former prisoner-of-war barracks that had been transported from Missouri to Notre Dame after the war. TACKLING NOTRE DAME's poignantly peak moments, interspersed with interludes of daffy desperation, stretch beyond Vetville and ultimately across eighteen years when finally, the Ph.D. and the Ph.T. are realized.

Notre Dame Stadium as seen from the 13th floor of the library.
Photo by Brother Martinus Bombardier, C.S.C.

I
Enterprisingly Yours

Suppose you were busily making supper with the "help" of your fifteen month old daughter, when your husband came home from work with his empty lunch bucket in one hand, application papers for admittance to Notre Dame's graduate school in the other and said:

"History has always been my first love. I want to quit my job and go to Notre Dame for a Master's and then a Ph.D. degree so I can become a history professor at a college or university. I have an insatiable desire to investigate Napoleon's Egyptian Campaign, and I have always wanted to delve into Hapsburg Dominions on the Abdication of Charles V in 1556. Can you understand?"

Could I understand?

With a courtship under my belt that had been shared in turn with Alexander the Great, Julius Caesar, the Huns, Henry VIII, and Patrick Henry, — could I understand?

Could I understand, — I who spent my honeymoon with Commodore Perry gliding serenely over the waves of Lake Erie, and who, because of Anthony's obsession, associated the word "charge" with Pickett at Missionary Ridge or Teddy Roosevelt at

San Juan Hill, instead of how to proceed at the local department store.

Could I understand, — when I was the co-owner of a Charles of London couch in the living room, a warming pan in the bedroom, a colonial recipe for gingerbread in the kitchen, and the personal papers of Douglas Haig in the bathroom? Yes, I could understand.

"If you want to be a history professor, I guess we'll manage somehow. Besides, I have always wanted to know more about Hapsburg Dominions on the Abdication of Charles V in 1556," I replied, crossing my fingers.

And so we filled out the papers and Anthony was eventually accepted at the University of Notre Dame's graduate school. The year was 1951, and because Lieutenant j.g. Black had served in the U.S. Navy, the G.I. Bill would be the passport to higher education.

"I'll get part-time jobs," Anthony proffered.

"And I'll help, too," I put in, and together we made plans to tackle Notre Dame.

Notice was given to the manager of the Pennsylvania steel mill that Anthony's job as a time clerk would soon be available to someone else.

When moving day came, we put the lunch bucket in a plastic bag and packed all other household necessities into our five-year-old Chevy.

The ironing board, however, offered considerable resistance. Because it ran the entire length of the car, it kept Anthony and me separated for the entire trip. It was almost as though we were part of a Quaker congregation of 1795. Tiny Stephanie, however, bridged the divider with great agility, creating havoc on both sides. But no matter which side of the ironing board you happened to be on, it was clear we had plucked our roots severely, for, as we headed into Hoosierland, we had no job, no contacts, and little money. Acceptance to the graduate school at Notre Dame was the only kernel on our particular stalk of wheat.

But what had we to worry about? Hadn't my grandmother known famine in Ireland? Hadn't she, Rose Gribben, survived the rigors of life in Portglenone, County Antrim, before coming to the United States? And hadn't Anthony's forbearers made it across the sea from Ireland, too, only to die when the boat docked at Baltimore, leaving three children to make it on their own? After mulling over all the possibilities and impossibilities, one thing was certain. We would succeed, or die in the attempt. What we didn't know then was that it would take us eighteen years to accomplish our goal.

Although I knew my future role would be the same as in the past, keeping the dishes washed and caring for baby Stephanie, I determined I would do all I could to earn my Ph.T. (the honorary "degree" that accompanies any husband or wife's Ph.D., and which means "Putting him or her Through.")

Now the beautiful campus of the University of Notre Dame spread before us. How could you not succeed in a place like this? Notre Dame, in the summer of 1951, was a sun-filled, greenly-serene paradise. The reflective lakes offered double exposure to the beautiful buff buildings, and the

4

spirituality of the place leaped out with
startling impact. Black-cassocked priests reading
their breviaries paced amid the mallards at
water's edge, and the tips of the willows, gently
stroking the shallows, disturbed nothing at all.
The spire from Sacred Heart Church, which housed
the lofty clock and monastery bells, spindled up
toward the heavens, and the Lady of the Golden
Dome, Notre Dame, ever-vigilant, was Mother of
all. The Grotto, a replica of the one at Lourdes,
held the tapers of a myriad of prayers, and daily
communicants among the students were as numerous
as swallows at Capistrano on any March 19th.

Students belonged to various clubs and
participated in them as now, in the mock political
conventions, in the rap sessions in the Huddle,
the annual Mardi Gras, and the An Toastal
Celebration-of-Spring weekend. In those days, "in
loco parentis" was rigidly pursued by the priest-
rectors in the various halls, and "Black Mack" -
Father Charles McCarragher, C.S.C., Prefect of
Discipline, reigned supreme.

In 1951 the Campus basked in the shadow of Our
Lady, and a spread-out cleanness carpeted the very
footpaths. The saucer magnolias, pink nature
jewels, less mature than now, stood as welcoming
sentinels on either side of the Administration
Building, and held out beckoning arms to Anthony
and me.

No doubt some of the beautiful hemlock and
Austrian pine trees dated back to 1841, when
Father Edward Sorin and his little band of six
brothers settled in the mother house of the
Community of Holy Cross at Notre Dame. Innumerable

***The famous Golden Dome atop the Administration Building at
Notre Dame University with the statue of Sacred Heart of
Jesus in the foreground.***

Photo by Brother Martinus Bombardier, C.S.C.

Left to right: Sacred Heart Church, Washington Hall and the Administration Building.

Photo by Brother Martinus Bombardier, C.S.C.

The Grotto at Notre Dame; an exact replica of the one at Lourdes, France.

Photo by Brother Martinus Bombardier, C.S.C.

junipers, ginkgos, and tall oaks were in evidence
in the 50's, and in the 1980's - river birches,
pin oaks and mountain ash as well. The trees had
witnessed it all: the rise of this great
University out of the swamp lands of the Mid-West,
the plain little log chapel, the Administration
Building, the forming of the magnificent lakes,
the dining halls, dormitories, the classroom
buildings, Stepan Center, the Memorial Library,
the high-rise student quarters, the Athletic and
Convocation Center, Moreau Seminary, Holy Cross
House . . . the physical plant, Notre Dame, was,
and is, breathtaking!

This was not the case, however, with our first
home in Indiana. The housing shortage was acute,
and after exhausting every lead we settled for a
trailer, an old mobile home, parked about fifteen
miles from Notre Dame in a patch of green near
Lakeville, Indiana. "Home" was a living room,
kitchen and bedroom, with one unconnected
bathroom, a blatant study in unadulterated
uselessness! Pipes that went absolutely nowhere
jutted from the walls. The sink faucets gleamed
promisingly in the florescent lighting, but nary a
trickle of water traversed through. It was a
corpse of a bathroom, with no life in its veins, a
make-believe facade from the Land of Pretend.

Reality was out yonder, an out-house complete
with cobwebs. Two whole weeks of this travesty
were endured before a three-room furnished
apartment opened up in the nearby town of
Mishawaka. Named for an Indian princess, Mishawaka
is a pleasantly clean community that receives
national prizes for its fastidious neatness.

The Log Chapel is a favorite place for N.D. grads to marry.
Built in 1686 and rebuilt in 1831, it formerly was used as a
mission church for area Indians.
Photo by Brother Martinus Bombardier, C.S.C.

We settled in.

As long as Anthony succeeded in finding part-time jobs to supplement his G.I. Bill, we made sweeping scholastic progress. But during the in-between times, the no-job, worrisome periods, his educational drive would lag and he would threaten to give up the long haul. "I'd better forget about history and think about making some money," he'd say. "We have to eat, you know."

But Anthony would make a whale-of-a-professor, and I knew it. "What could I do to keep him in school?" I asked myself over and over again.

Spenser Wilkinson, a British military strategist, had written years before: "The path to great achievements runs along the brink of the abyss." And so it was, our so-called "brinkmanship" was steadily recognized. We had only to make a few pertinent choices to stay on the narrow path that led to his Ph.D. If we chose knowledge, we could not have security. If we bought books, we could not buy bricks. There were decisions to make. "Brinkmanship" had its price. And, with a little one to worry about, the price was steeper than ever.

But suddenly, penetrating through the worry, came a beam of light that scattered the darkness. Studebaker was hiring! Voila! Assembly-line workers were needed at once. The educational momentum was again at full speed ahead. But, oh, the hours, the shifts, the working around the academic schedule! And what exactly did an automobile upholsterer do for a living?

Armed with an apronful of tacks, clutching a magnetic hammer, and fortified with diligent

*The University of Notre Dame Library houses 1.5 million
volumes; on the very spot where Vetville once stood.*
Photo by Brother Martinus Bombardier, C.S.C.

determination, Anthony would sprint onto the
conveyor belt and into a newly-formed Studebaker,
whereupon he would begin formulating the car's
"innards."

He had learned his job well.

"You cram tacks in your mouth," the foreman had
told him, "and you spit them out onto the magnetic
hammer. See? One atta time. You need to keep one
hand free to hold the material and the other hand
to hammer with."

"But what if I swallow the tacks?" asked
Anthony.

"Nothing to worry about. Digestive juices
dissolve tacks!" the foreman reassured.

The weeks of working until three a.m. (while
attending classes at Notre Dame at eight a.m.)
turned into months. Then, suddenly the boom-bubble
burst. Several thousand men, including Anthony,
were forced into the ranks of the unemployed.
Whether the South Bend Chamber of Commerce wanted
to admit it or not, the city was having a
recession and jobs were non-existent.

Here was my first real chance to do something
concrete towards my Ph.T. "Listen, Anthony . . .,"
I began, pushing his hair back. "Your losing this
job is probably the best thing that ever happened,
because now you can devote full time to studying
for your degree and I'll earn the money." It was a
wonderfully impractical idea and his eyes told me
so.

Magnanimously, he patted my arm and said
quietly, "You take care of the baby and stay out
of trouble. I'll find something."

But while he was trying, there was tuition to be

paid, baby food to be bought, rent to be scraped together, and no job!

"One thing," I kept reassuring, "you've got job experience. You'll find a job. I know you will."

And finally, this jack-of-all-trade experience paid off, for Anthony found employment as a part-time janitor at Notre Dame. He had exchanged his magnetic hammer for a broom. Along with the new job came, understandably, a strictly restricted budget which one unnecessary orange popsicle could throw out of whack! And so the days became one long string of spaghetti after the other, until one morning, when the sun came up with a bounce.

"I've got a job!" I announced grandly. "I'm going to sell linens to prospective brides!" I was enthusiastic! At that moment I could have sold a ton of cigarettes to the lung division of the American Cancer Society! "Beautiful table linens!" I continued, "an ice blue dinner cloth, a pale green damask, an Irish linen . . . "

Anthony brought his fist down hard on the formica-topped table. "How do you expect to sell tablecloths, my good woman," he said in grandiose fashion, "when you so seldom use one?"

But I didn't have time to quibble. I was meeting my first prospective customer that very afternoon, and my sales talk was as full of blanks as the Watergate tapes. I had to rewrite it. I had to rehearse. I had to throttle my pounding heart.

Later that afternoon, as appointment time drew near, I re-examined my sample case while waiting for Anthony and the car. Smoothing and unsmoothing the cloths, reciting aloud to myself, I kept one eye on the clock, and the other on little

Stephanie who threatened to dump the merchandise kerflooey.

As I snapped the lock on my heavy suitcase full of samples, Anthony, like an unsuccessful genie, appeared, without the car! "It broke down!" he panted. "It's in a garage. Call a cab!"

"A cab???" I exasperated. "When I haven't even made a sale?"

"Take it out of the profits," Anthony said glumly and reached for the phone.

When the taxi arrived, Anthony patted me and the linens affectionately, wished us the best of luck, and hurried us to our respective places in the cab. "To the South Shore Station," I told the cabbie breathlessly, "and please hurry!"

I was meeting a bride-to-be at the train station because it was convenient for both of us, and because she had requested that I not come to her home since she lived with her aging grandmother who did not approve of her spending good money on even groceries, let alone fancy linens. The Women's Lounge at the station would provide ample room for the linen display, and we would be far from the peering eyes of her disapproving grandmother.

I settled back into the cab. How to begin my talk? My thoughts concentrated on the sales pitch. Five minutes later, as we neared the station, the driver, who had been quiet the whole trip, suddenly shouted. "Lady! There she is!"

"Yes," I heartily agreed. There was the station, big as life.

"You'd better pay me now," he said hurriedly.

The dollar was easy to locate in my many-sectioned purse, but just as I came up with two quarters, three dimes and four nickels, the cab jolted to an abrupt stop. The money flew north, south, east and west!

"Oh-h-h-h-h-h Lady," moaned the cabbie, adding, "here, I'll help." I was searching under the back seat for the last coin when I heard him say in a solemn tone, "Here. Put this on the train. She'll be there in a jiffy!"

I righted myself, flabbergasted and taut as a porcupine quill. It had happened! The cabdriver had given my precious sample case to a porter with running legs who was making off with my beautiful linens!

"Oh, how could you?" I screamed at the cabbie, while taking off in pursuit of my case! "Stop! Stop!" I kept shouting at the porter. "I'm not going anywhere!"

But the noise from the train was too much and the porter's legs were too fast. From somewhere behind, the cabdriver kept shrieking, "You'll make it! You'll make it!" Then came the thundering shudder as the train began to move!

In spite of the fact that I "kicked" in the final stretch, I lost the race. The linen sample case had disappeared completely into the shadows of the train. I had to give up, in deference to my pounding heart.

"She's all taken care of, honey," the porter proudly shouted over the din.

Smiling now from the rapidly moving steps was an eager-looking conductor. "Here, grab my hand," he yelled. I weakly extended one arm, and then held on hard. "I haven't had a train ride in years," I thought to myself as I was hoisted aboard to reclaim my expensive linens.

It was hours later, under the encouraging glow of the kitchen light, that I came to the conclusion that the life of a saleswoman was just too indefinite a way of making a few dollars.

"You just never know how a sale will turn out," I mused.

"Or what state you'll end up in," Anthony muttered, tired from his journey of retrieving me. Then he continued in a sympathetic tone, "Why don't you just stay home and quit worrying? I'll find some kind of extra work to do besides the janitor job."

"On which days do you have only one class?"

"On Tuesdays and Thursdays. But why do you want to know that?"

"Well, then, why don't I put my name in to do substitute teaching on those days, while you watch Stephanie?"

"You mean the regular teachers have to confine themselves to having the flu only on Tuesdays and Thursdays?" he asked pessimistically. "Look," he continued, "Stephanie needs you at home."

That was a good point. If only I could find something to do at home that carried some renumeration with it.

"Just stay home," Anthony urged. "We'll manage somehow."

"I just might," I answered. "You know, I've been thinking about entering those contests that are always advertised. You know, the twenty-five word statements and slogans." As I further explained all the money they give away every year, I was suddenly caught up in the enthusiasm of a new enterprise, in spite of the fact that by this time, my future professor was finding the Napoleonic Wars far more interesting.

By dinner time the next evening, things looked as bright as a new tulip on a May morning.

"What's for supper?" Anthony called as he came in the apartment door.

"Noodle-ee-doo," I replied, not batting an eye. There was a silence. Only the "Noodle-ee-doo" simmered embarrassedly in the oven.

Finally Anthony's head appeared around the white-enameled kitchen door. "What is Noodle-ee-doo?" he asked with great intensity.

"Well, it's a big piece of dough — a big noodle — with a ground meat mixture inside and it's twisted 'round and 'round a cake tube pan. When it's baked you pour a tomato sauce mixture over it," I chattered, afraid to pause.

"And where did you acquire this ingenious recipe?" he inquired.

"Well, it's my recipe. I made it up. I have to have an original idea for a baking contest, to win $25,000." There, it was out.

"Your recipe!" he laughed, and then he kissed me solidly. I returned the affection, knowing full well it would have to last through to the last crumb of Noodle-ee-doo.

About a week later, "Tropical Treasure" made its appearance. It was tasty — at the beginning, coconut pressed into the dough of a pie crust shell, baked, and then filled with a mixture of vanilla pudding, chopped dates and crushed pineapple. Every recipe needs perfecting, and so I tested and retested. But finding a "Tropical Treasure" almost every night of the week became as unbearable as it was unpalatable. And, to be sure, not a coin tinkled in the pie pan from this supreme effort. The judging agency was unimpressed.

I then tried "Carrara Sugar Cubes" which were marbled squares of angel food batter, dark and light, baked in refrigerator ice cube trays, and iced with confectioner's frosting.

When "Flying Saucer Marble Cake" landed on our table, I felt that it was a sure thing. The recipe had a surprise twist to it! Just before a very-ordinary chocolate batter was poured into baking pans, little vanilla wafers were added and then baked right along with the cake. When the cake was cut, the little yellow sections resembled saucers — all flying at different angles!

"See!" I proudly exlaimed to Anthony and Stephanie.

Neither said a word.

And the "Flying Saucer Marble Cake" failed to fly us to the pot of gold at the end of the rainbow.

But one day Anthony made a constructive contribution. "Cut up bits of marshmallow," he said confidentially. "Put them into a devil's food batter and call it 'Midnight Blizzard'!"

"Wonderful!" I cried and a few hours later, with a big brown-handled knife in tow, we embarked on an exciting adventure.

"Cut straight down the middle!" I said.

"Why, it looks like an ordinary chocolate cake!" he said in a disappointed tone.

Virginia whipping up a winner.

"Try cutting across!" I said, hoping the result would be different.

Anthony cut but the blizzard had disappeared. Anthony sat down to think it over. In a tremendous heap on the table before him were millions of chocolate crumbs. "It seems," he finally said in a slow, deliberate tone, "that there has been a Great Thaw."

"We'll get an idea yet," I soothed.

"Not I. This," he gestured with the knife, pointing to the dark heap, "is my swan song." And he went back to Napoleon.

But I would not give up. Strong determination, coupled with a complete lack of know-how in the art of baking, put me in the uncomplimentary position of scraping the bottom of the culinary barrel. "Grapefruit Upside Down Cake" put in its brief appearance, along with a one-night stand of "Celery Soup Bread."

Then one cold, snowy evening a $25,000 thought came to me. "Wouldn't it be wonderful," I thought out loud, "to develop a pop-corn cookie? Mix the batter, sprinkle in the corn, then read a book while the melodious little 'pops' talked back as the cookies baked!"

The inspiration was electrifying. I chose a chocolate cookie batter so that the contrast between the white popcorn and dark cookie would be all the more striking.

With feet propped, a book to read and an apple to eat, I waited eagerly, my ears trained for that certain sound I would hear momentarily.

The cookies finished baking without a single pop. I turned the dial slowly upward until the

five hundred degrees mark was reached. Still no
"pop." The cookies were burned at the edges, but
the popcorn kernels were still as hard as a new
tile floor. Failure again!

"I'll never, never enter another baking
contest," I sniffled, exasperated.

"It's all right; it's all right," Anthony
soothed. "You're just learning the hard way."

"But I just discovered something that any, any
jackass should have known all along," I choked,
probing my humility. "You bake cookies at three
hundred degrees and you need very, very hot
temperatures for popcorn! Oh-h-h I've wasted so
much food!" and I collapsed in Anthony's arms.
"You try too hard," Anthony reasoned. "Why don't
you quit trying?"

"I can't," I said, thinking of all the eggs I
had stored in the refrigerator. "I'm too
involved."

A few soaked handkerchiefs and a couple of days
later, "Custard Loaf Cake" was brought into being.
But from the difficulty I had with the custard
always forgetting to stay custard and trespassing
into cake, and vice versa, I knew that it was
extremely doubtful whether the judges would give
the nod to such an vascillating concoction!

Cinerama inspired "Cinna-Lemma" cake, a three-
dimensional two-layered specialty that featured
three important ingredients: cinnamon, lemon
juice, and the necessary-to-enter-the contest-
ingredient, flour.

While waiting for the outcome of this entry, I
decided to abandon baking contests for a time and
concentrate on the twenty-five word statement

type, the kind that start with "I like so and so, whatever it is, because . . . ."

"Get a new gimmick to your entry," Anthony suggested, "and I'll wager you'll win one yet."

An orange juice contest was occupying all my attention at present. "I like such and such orange juice because . . . ."

"The only thing an orange is good for," Anthony said, "is a good squeeze."

The deadline was drawing near, and I hadn't decided on what to send in, but finally it came to me:

"I squeeze only my husband and still serve the best-tasting, no-waste, vitamin-packed orange juice on the market . . . ." and the rest praised the specific brand name.

Six weeks later the entry brought an electric powered toy automobile that retailed for four hundred dollars!

"You did it!" Anthony congratulated.

"We'll sell it," I said.

"Wa-ah!" Stephanie cried.

"We'll save it, 'til she's ready." Father had settled it.

No matter how I figured it, we couldn't eat that aquamarine fiber-glass car. But just looking at it gave us a lift and for a few days anyway, our financial future looked all rosy, with an aquamarine glow around the edges.

II
Vetville, Notre Dame

The reality of my helping to bring home the bacon and earning the Ph.T., was certainly beset with obstacles. Anthony's Ph.D., however, was coming along. His language requirements of French and German had been fulfilled, and, best news of all, we were given the green light to move into Vetville, a barracks housing development provided by Notre Dame for married students and their wives. And, all because we now had 1 3/4 children, — the requisite being two.

The barracks, which had been used to house Japanese prisoners of war in Missouri, had been secured from the United States Government, free of charge except for transportation costs. Notre Dame contracted to ship thirty-eight units, which in turn would accommodate one hundred fourteen Notre Dame student-families. Our unit apartment was numbered 35-A. We now had a living room, kitchen, two bedrooms, one bath, and two underground garbage cans, — all for thirty-three dollars a month!

A few weeks later, I had the new baby. This one, a lovely boy, was named Robert Joseph after his paternal grandfather. The moment I had waited for

23

THIS AREA WAS THE SITE OF VETVILLE, MARRIED STUDENT HOUSING 1945 – 1962

MANY WERE THE TRIALS — THANKS TO THE HOLY FAMILY FOR THE MANY BLESSINGS NEEDED TO PERSEVERE

Photo by Brother Martinus Bombardier, C.S.C.

A few Vetville units photographed in 1961 by the South Bend Tribune

had finally come. Since I was the second of three daughters, I grew up in a world completely devoid of boys. It was so minus the opposite sex that I hadn't the slightest idea of what little boys looked like. But, I decided, I would eventually solve the mystery by someday having a baby boy myself. And now it was done.

Stephanie was happy in the knowledge that now she had a playmate and planned for the day when they could play house together. The new baby had Stephanie's blond hair and fair coloring, but unlike her, was not the wriggling handful of protoplasm she had been. He was cuddly and contented. Was it because he was a second baby or could it be that he had a different temperament?

Just minutes after Robbie was born, a letter was delivered to our apartment unit telling us that we had yet another mouth to feed, that of a cocker spaniel, the spaniel being a minor award in a contest that I had entered months before.

"The things I have won are all well and good," I said to Anthony, dangling my feet over the side of the hospital bed, "but we need cold, hard cash, and I haven't won any."

"You're doing very well," he consoled. "Both mother and baby are doing well. And father sweeps a mean broom," he concluded grandly, using an imaginary broom for effect.

Three months after we had moved into Vetville Anthony was asked to run for the council.

"There is no pay for councilman," Anthony explained, "but the Mayor of Vetville gets free rent. Maybe I can work up to that."

We didn't know that practically everyone in the

tiny community, at one time or another, had run for something. We also didn't know that most men in Vetville, who were busy with books while simultaneously trying to earn a living, did their best to avoid these non-paying jobs and pushed them on to newcomers.

Anthony's campaign speech was a brief one and centered on Vetville's unpaved main thoroughfare, Hesburgh Way, which was dubbed after the President of the University. His campaign pledge was: "Elect me and I will fill in the holes on our road."

His opponent's campaign pledge was: "Elect me and I will pave Hesburgh Way," and as it turned out, this proved to be the winning slogan.

After the election, we realized Anthony's pledge should have been: "Elect me and I will get a phone for every apartment." Due to a shortage of phones and our lack of seniority, we had to share a phone with a neighbor. We wore a path across the street calling possible employers in seeking work. Any kind of work!

By now, however, it was not just our nerves that were becoming frayed at the edges. Anthony's pants were also sporting two good sized holes. I noticed the holes one day as Anthony dashed out the door in response to word that he had a long distance phone call waiting for him in the unit across the street. Minutes later he returned with a sober look on his face. As he came through the door he said very quietly and deliberately, trying to restrain his temper — "Look, I don't ask much of life, or of you, for that matter, but the least you could do would be to tell me when my backside is sticking out!"

In the weeks that followed, we attended a pot
luck supper for Vetvillers, and nursed Stephanie
and Robbie through the measles. Being unemployed,
we had more time than usual to study our
environment. We discovered that Vetville, a
treeless, cindery domain, was an interesting
place, and like all little communities it had its
"Marilyn Monroe," its town gossip, its joiners,
its organizers, and, its pains-in-the-neck. On the
other hand, it had its abundance of sympathetic,
intelligent wives and devoted mothers helping
their husbands who were slowly working their way
through undergraduate and graduate programs at
Notre Dame.

"How to Save Money" and "How to Earn Money" were
favorite topics for discussion in Vetville and we
consoled ourselves with the fact that we were not
alone in our struggle.

One wife held that she partially solved the
problem of their scanty income by making her own
popsicles. Another firmly believed in the rotation
of sheets as her budget panacea. (This week the
smaller hem is at the top, next week, it's at the
bottom.) Powdered milk had its devotees, and
nowhere in the world could more knowledge be
exchanged on budgets and bridge than at the
Veterans' Recreation Center at the edge of the
little community. For twenty-five cents, one could
learn the latest thinking of Goren and Culbertson,
play progressive bridge for three hours, compete
for lovely prizes donated by local merchants, and
perceive what was needed in this post-World-War II
educational settlement.

While the fathers of the area were pursuing
education and culture at the University, a handful

of mothers attended local business college classes
as well as night classes at Indiana University,
South Bend campus. But what about our preschoolers? Were these children culturally-
deprived? What about a little school for them?

In the years I was growing up, I had attended
the unique dancing school of a most unusual and
eccentric woman. Her studio was perched directly
beside the Baltimore and Ohio railroad tracks at
McKeesport, Pennsylvania. It was often difficult
to follow the steps, the music, or the spoken
directions for that matter, as freight trains
rumbled by.

But the most startling oddity about her place of
business was that her Christmas decorations were
on display almost year round. The decorations
consisted of tinsel, icicles, red and green sweeps
and ornaments hanging on them, be it December or
May. This idiosyncrasy was explained by those who
loved and understood her by pointing out that she
was a connoisseur of beauty in general and
Christmas in particular, and she just couldn't
bear to take the sparkling things down.

Her grit, determination, and, above all, her
tremendous imagination, were rarities. Her
favorite words were "spectacular" and "the show
was the thing!" She inspired her pupils to "reach
for the stars" in dancing and in life, and her
teachings did not fall on barren ground.

My mind was made up. Vetville needed a little
dancing school for the children.

The Councilmen of Vetville approved of my use of
the Veterans' Recreation Hall free of charge for a
dancing school. Since all of the children's

fathers were students at the University, most of them on the G.I. Bill, I set my fee at only twenty-five cents for each half-hour session. Thirty pupils responded, from the ages of three to ten.

Their quarters managed to pay for the parade of piano players that came and went, as their classes at Notre Dame demanded, and also for my very dear friend, Evelyn, who took care of my own children.

Everything tapped along smoothly enough for a time. I was actually making a profit! Then an epidemic of measles struck down three-fourths of my dancing school, and along with it, my profits. My students and I finally made it through the epidemic and moved into rehearsals for the spring recital.

Our spring recital was presented in the Notre Dame Law Auditorium, complete with gypsies, flowers, elves, four-year-old "can-can" girls, The Swanee River devotees, and all "Les Etoiles" in general, and they tripped off the stage after their final curtain call to a tremendous round of applause. But at the end of our spectacular spring recital, I found that my dance school adventure had put me fifteen dollars and seventy-five cents in the hole. It was a lot of fun, but as far as making money, I told Anthony, "I'm jinxed and besides that, I'm exhausted."

To which he replied, "And you're also broke."

I thought that perhaps I should go back to entering contests, but that was so indefinite and sweepstakes were taking over the field. Maybe I should do some other kind of writing. Come to think of it, I had sold an article once.

The article was written in anger, mailed in haste, and sold for fifteen dollars to a baby magazine shortly after Stephanie had arrived. It had to do with the mental aspects of pregnancy, a mother-to-be's emotions, attitudes and feelings while awaiting her baby. It particularly concerned the tactlessness of doctors who plague pregnant women with questions like: "What did you have for lunch last Tuesday, a lettuce leaf? I thought so! You know you're eating too much."

My own obstetrician had upset me so terribly each time I went for a check-up, that after each visit, I would leave his office, head for the nearest rest room, enter a stall and stand there bawling until my Kleenex supply ran out. I would then resort to toilet tissue, sob a while longer, dry my tears and head for home.

"You've gained three and one half pounds!" he would say, aghast. "You were told to gain only three. Why can't you control yourself?" If I ate, I was scolded. If I didn't eat, I was scolded. Mentally I experienced a tremendous amount of anguish the whole nine months. Nobody, but nobody, had ever been so weak, so hungry, and so-o-o-o pregnant!

How completely relieved I was when, in my hour of need, I was wheeled into the delivery room and told that my O.B. was out of town. I was jubilant at the discovery that I had finally escaped his clutches! Let the trash man, the nurse's aid, the window-washer assist me! My timing was perfect. I had, in the end, outwitted my antagonizer.

Months later, I wrote all my anguished pregnancy down on paper. When I succeeded in finding a publisher for my article, I sent the dear doctor a copy of the magazine with the notation:

"The piece that begins on page nineteen concerns you. It is hoped you will profit from its reading." What I really wanted to say was, "the piece that begins on page nineteen concerns you, you big overgrown bully!" but prudence triumphed.

"Sure, you have writing talent," Anthony proffered. "Remember what the prof wrote on the paper you did for me when I was tacking my way upholstering Studebakers?"

Yes, I remembered. Because Anthony was getting home from the factory at 3 a.m. and had classes beginning at 8 a.m., I had foolishly volunteered to write his term paper on the subject of "Iconoclasm in the Latter Byzantine Empire." It was returned with a note scrawled across the title page which read, "Interesting, readable, but not very deep."

The professor was so right. I had delved into that subject with all the enthusiasm of a vegetarian giraffe watching a sluggish earthworm's meanderings from a height of twenty-four feet!

"You just didn't feel deeply enough about Iconoclasm in the Latter Byzantine Empire, that's all," husband-dear chided. There was only one thing I was feeling at the moment, extreme fatigue from trying to keep the house in order when two tiny children had only one thing on their minds — disorder!

So consequently, the first renewed literary attempt was a short essay on the contrast between a harassed mother's housekeeping and the quiet serenity that exists in a convent; how the nuns have a place for everything and once that place is established for each object, order pervaded for all eternity. The article, which brought fifteen dollars (the magic number), was entitled: "Convents are Clean." But before it was published in a small Catholic periodical, several advance advertising notices about the article found their way into our weekly Catholic newspaper which read:

"A housewife asks the question — ARE CONVENTS CLEAN?"

I pictured indignant Mother Superiors from all parts of the country beating a path to my door to inspect my own housekeeping. But for all my imagining, nary a letter, pro or con, came from even one tiny postulant, let alone an esteemed Mother Superior.

The next article I turned out was published in the now defunct AVE MARIA, and entitled "One Thousand and One Ways of Fixing Hamburger."

Anthony, who will never read mere copy but only the printed published word, angrily said, "But you've exaggerated. You'd think we never ate anything but hamburger!"

"Well . . .," I argued.

It was Anthony who contributed the idea for the next article when he asked, "Why don't you write something about the Notre Dame football team from a woman's viewpoint?"

We knew the majority of the players well. In fact, some of them used to baby-sit for us occasionally. Baby-sit? That was it! Football players as baby-sitters would make a terrific article. The title was Anthony's: "Notre Dame Football Players Aren't So Tough!"

34

In the article I depicted the Notre Dame iron-
men of the gridiron in a less publicized role,
that of baby-sitter. Underneath all the padding
and muscles the football players had hearts that
responded to a little tyke slurping on his or her
bottle.

Several couples in our little community
volunteered information and pictures of players
who were friends and baby-sitters for their
children while I arranged for a professional
photographer to get shots of other football
players baby-sitting.

This time, LOOK magazine was interested, but
they politely informed me that my pictures were
not good enough. "No one," they said over the
phone from New York, "can take pictures like we
can." I heartily agreed, as I couldn't afford not
to.

Soon, two photographers from the magazine were
winging their way to South Bend. In the meantime,
I starched my children's rompers and put an extra
twist in Robbie's hair.

When the lovely people from New York arrived in
South Bend, they came first to say hello to us and
then proceeded to the practice field to shoot
pictures of the players in action. They wanted
shots proving how tough they were before they took
pictures of them as baby-sitters.

In order for the photographers to get on the
scrimmage field, they sought permission from the
Notre Dame football officials who immediately
expressed their disapproval of such an article.
"This isn't the right time for a piece on a
subject like that!" they exclaimed. "This is going
to be a losing season."

PAUL HORNING, quarterback, babysits Chrissie Nicholson.
After graduation Horning went on to become the great star of
the Green Bay Packers.
Photo by Wally Kunkle

RAY LEMEK, captain of the 1955 N.D. team with Stephanie and Robbie Black.

Photo by Richard Uschold

***DON SCHAEFER**, fullback, playing with the Black children.
Don later played professionally for the Philadelphia Eagles.*
Photo by Wally Kunkle

JIM MORSE, halfback, with wife Leah Rae and their little girl Barbara.

Photo by Wally Kunkle

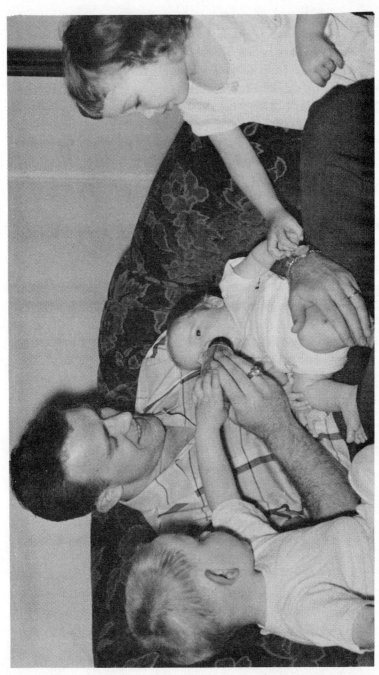

JOE HEAP, halfback, with Joanne, Richard and Mike Uschold. Joe later played for the New York Giants.

Photo by Richard Uschold

The players were instructed to say they were not interested in posing for pictures and I was given an appointment to discuss my article with the team's head sports-writer.

With his hat on the back of his head, my host leaned cautiously over his desk toward me and said in a low, confidential tone, "How would you feel, Mrs. Black, if the fans would suddenly start yelling from the bleachers — 'we want the baby-sitters'?"

Two days later the photographers flew back to New York without the story and I went back to the kids' room to do some ironing. For my time, money for pictures, and wasted energy, all I had to show for it was a nervous stomach.

Two weeks later, however, a check for one hundred dollars arrived, along with my article, "Notre Dame Football Players Aren't So Tough." The notation on the check read, "For preliminary work" and a letter was enclosed expressing regrets that the article had been squelched.

"How's my poor wife?" Anthony called when he got home from class.

"Not so poor," I answered, waving a check under his nose.

"You are a successful author," he commented. "You don't even break into print and you're paid for it! One hundred dollars was three months Vetville's rent! Bonanza!

III
Fertile Valley, U.S.A.

Our Vetville was a vibrant little community
whose many offspring earned it the title "Fertile
Valley." Almost everyone blamed the prolific
number of children on the amount of peanut butter
that was consumed for economic purposes. One
mother-in-law, helping out again for the fifth
time in the new-baby-period, put it this way:
"It's because these men use only their heads,
going to school. If they used their backs as well
on hard labor jobs, they wouldn't have so much
energy left at night!"

When summer came upon us in "Fertile Valley,"
talk of "The Strawberry King" again reared its
head.

"If I could just get enough money together to
rent a truck," Anthony lamented, "I'd go to
Michigan and get some of those strawberries. You
know, Benton Harbor isn't far, only about thirty
miles, and then I'd drive the berries to
Pennsylvania." Anthony had a customer or two lined
up in Pennsylvania who said they would buy them,
but the lack of cold cash always prevented the
scheme from materializing.

Fortunately, dust kept accumulating at Notre

Dame's Administration Building and the janitor's
job that Anthony held there remained intact.
During summer vacation it became a once a week
clean-up instead of a daily endeavor, but one
day's work was better than none.

One of the students Anthony worked with at the
janitorial job was a Nigerian who came to the
United States to study at the University. He and
his wife had decided to leave their children in
Africa while he was going through school and that
gave her plenty of extra time to help out wherever
she was needed. They were not accustomed to our
ways of living and continued to practice their own
customs. He would bring his wife along to "help"
do the janitorial work. She would enter the
Administration Building, always one or two steps
behind him with a vacuum cleaner slung over her
shoulder, buckets in one hand and mops in the
other. Then, while her husband sat at a desk
"studying," his wife would clean office after
office.

Anthony often chided me about the Nigerian
couple, and say, "Why don't you come over and help
me sweep?"

Finally, several Vetville wives got through to
the gracious Nigerian woman and explained the ways
of American living. They realized that she had
learned the American way of doing things when one
of the Vetville residents asked her to help with
some house-cleaning and she said she would be glad
to do the work, but she didn't know what to
charge.

When the Vetville wife said, "Ask your husband
and see what he thinks is a fair sum," the

Nigerian woman stiffened and, in an almost American accent, said, "My husband does not need to know."

When summer was at its fullest, a polio scare enveloped our little Vetville community. Six children, three from Vetville itself, and three from adjacent areas had contracted the dread disease. The local hospital, with straight pins representing each case on a huge wall map, had tabbed these six cases "epidemic proportions." Whenever possible, residents were leaving Vetville and going home to parents and grand-parents, with little tykes in tow.

It was during the polio scare that the University, with umpteen barrels of nails and boxes of shingles, embarked on a beautify and insulate Vetville project. Ten Vetville fathers were hired to tack on the light green, dark brown, or in-between wine colored shingle-sidings, and Anthony was one of the lucky ones! The job would last until all one-hundred and fourteen apartment units were finished.

Tying on his apron with its pockets stuffed with nails, Anthony said, "Don't you think, for the sake of the kids, you better get out of here and stay with your folks in Pennsylvania for a while?"

Since the medical profession knew so little about polio in those pre-Salk days, our imaginations worked overtime. I immediately agreed to take the kids to Grandma's. As soon as Anthony received his first week's paycheck, we bought a train ticket on the Baltimore and Ohio Railroad, left him with his nails in Indiana, and hid out in Pennsylvania.

44

Anthony kept us informed of the polio epidemic's
course. When we received the "all-clear" signal,
we returned to our home in Vetville to take up
living where we left off. Polio's aftermath left
only one little boy in a leg brace, which he
ultimately discarded. But there was a Vetville
father who would spend the rest of his life in a
wheelchair because of the dreaded affliction.

Anthony's hammering job lasted all summer. By
September, the former prisoner-of-war barracks
were all sporting new exteriors and the children,
in days to come, rushed to tell visiting
relatives, "My daddy did the green one, that red
one, that brown one, etc."

When classes resumed in the fall, Anthony was
informed that the University janitorial job was
still his.

"The offices I clean," he would boast, "are the
cleanest on the entire first floor of the
Administration building," and then he would swing
his imaginary broom.

The chaplain of our tiny college community was
the one person whom life seemed to hinge around. A
most conscientious priest, Father James Moran,
C.S.C., would visit the sick, baptize the newborn,
help find jobs for the unemployed, answer a myriad
of questions about practical as well as spiritual
matters, and come for coffee on late afternoons.
In addition to all of this, he was an accomplished
scholar of Latin and Greek, a university
professor, and a former president of Stonehill
College.

Little Stephanie resented his social visits
emphatically. "Stop talking to my mother," she

said one day while leaning on an arm of a chair
and looking directly into his face. This out-burst
was followed by, "Stop talking to Father Moran,
Mother."

Grabbing Stephanie by the sash on her dress, I
took her into the "crying room" (the bathroom) and
paddled her soundly. She remained in the "crying
room" until she stopped crying and was then
permitted to rejoin us.

Seconds after she made her re-entrance, Father
and I experienced the same thing all over again.

"Stop talking . . .," she said to the future
Dean of Admissions at Notre Dame. "Stop
talking . . .," she reiterated to me.

"What do I do now?" I asked Father Moran. I
thought he would remark that she was but a child,
that she was not really bothering him, and that
she would learn. But instead he said, "Whack her
again and put her in the crying room once and for
all!"

Hyper-active children were not diagnosed back in
the 1950's, but I am convinced that Stephanie was
one of them. Her brother, Robbie, was a snap
compared to her. I remember looking at him and
thinking, "What's wrong with you? You're no
trouble at all."

In spite of my having precious little time for
intellectual pursuits while contending with the
gyrations of two small children, I looked forward
to the stimulating conversations to be had at the
University history teas. Since, at Notre Dame, the
master's degree was a stepping stone to the Ph.D.,
we were currently living through the blood, sweat
and writing of Anthony's master's thesis, "The

Father James Moran, C.S.C.

Personal Relationship between England's Charles II
and Louis XIV of France," which covered the years
1660-1685. I was, by this time, versed exceedingly
well on these few years. But while sipping punch
with Notre Dame's Head-Of-The-History-Department,
I found I could discuss these years only so long.
When I got to the year 1686, my mind was a big
blank matched only by the reflection of my face in
the punch bowl.

And so it was that I attempted to plummet Father
Thomas McAvoy and myself into the present for
safer conversation. Clutching tenaciously at my
refreshment plate, I said, "Isn't this the most
insipid punch you've ever tasted, Father?"

The priest brightened instantly, raised his
bushy white eyebrows and said, "Oh, do you think
so?"

Thinking I had aroused his interest I continued,
telling him that one of the graduate students told
me how Father had always had the Star-lite
Restaurant cater his teas, and that frankly, I
thought they took advantage of his good nature
with this concoction. We talked on and on,
discussing the merits of using or not using
pineapple juice as a punch base. At the end of our
discussion, Father was off to circulate among his
guests.

It was just about one-half hour later that the
priest's greying secretary confided to me in
whispered tones, "You know, Father's so proud.
Proud as punch, you might say. This is the first
time he made the punch himself. He went downtown
in a taxi, got all the ingredients, and then mixed
them. Can you imagine? Father told me, 'I'm going

to give everyone a real treat for a change.'"
Then, with a tickled-pink shrug of her shoulders,
she remarked, "And, it's so delicious!"

The grandfather clock in the corner of the
drawing room bonged thunderously! The ice cubes
floating on the top of the pinkish brew began
whirling and twirling around in the great bowl as
Father-Head-Of-The-History-Department stirred his
latest contribution to humanity. And the red and
white carnation centerpiece seemed to wilt before
my very eyes!

I decided I had had it and reached for Anthony's
arm. As we tip-toed our way to the door, over the
soft oriental rug, past a bevy of heavily oiled
University past-presidents who stared forbiddingly
at us from their assigned places on the wall, the
Father-Head-Of-The-History-Department put down the
ladle, smiled, and waved a sporty good-bye.

I comforted myself by thinking life must go on,
while Anthony kept telling himself maybe he wasn't
really cut out to be an historian anyway.

Occasionally, and in spite of the "insipid"
punch, Anthony was given the opportunity to tutor
some undergraduate students in whatever field of
history they happened to be having difficulty.
When this happened, I casually threw in extra
meatballs to go with the spaghetti. Meatballs, in
prolific numbers, I discovered, were terrific
morale boosters. But then, too, an evening walk on
the beautiful Notre Dame campus also did wonders
for the spirit.

In the dusky half-light, when the lamps shone
yellow on the damp grass and the whole campus had
quit for the day, — this was my time for walking!

If there was a lecture in the Law Building's auditorium or in the adjacent Engineering Building, then the walk would have to be brisk. Or, if there was a play being presented in Washington Hall, you had to hurry! But if you wanted to soak in the spirit of the University, then you just stood beneath the Golden Dome and looked up. Our Lady, Notre Dame, was there, overseeing all.

A poetic Mayor of Vetville once said that he believed the Lady on the Golden Dome sometimes turned her head to look in the direction of Vetville. But it was common knowledge that those who wanted the Lady's undivided attention would go to the Notre Dame grotto where graduate Dr. Tom Dooley had prayed so often. The Blessed Mother always came through with a solution to a worrisome problem. The Mediatrix of all graces could be counted on for sure. She was the one who could always persuade her Divine Son. Hadn't we asked her to help us move into Vetville?

And Vetville, fittingly, had its real Christian. It was Nancy, very much in the minority (being a Methodist in a sea of Roman Catholics) who proved herself, time after time, the true Christ-bearer, the genuine Christopher. Was there a mother in Vetville confined to her bed with a threatening miscarriage? It was Nancy who would take her toddler children for long walks, buy them numerous ice cream cones, and start dinner so that it was well on its way by the time their father arrived home.

Was there a feverish child in Vetville? It was Nancy who offered her tiny fan to help cool the hot brow, even though the worn-out fan disturbed not a trickle of air as the age-darkened blades revolved haphazardly. But it was the only fan she had and she gave it.

Her cakes never rose to any occasion, but they were treasured by Vetvillers. A slice of her cake was a slice from a magnanimous heart. And it was Nancy who comforted when Anthony's father died suddenly back in Pennsylvania. He had simply walked out onto the back porch after dinner to see a new snowfall and collapsed at the age of fifty-nine.

It was while on the way back to Pennsylvania for the funeral (on money borrowed from Vetville's mayor) that Stephanie, responding to the hurried confusion of the moment, raised her little voice above the clickety-clacks of the train's wheels and philosophized, "Isn't it wonderful that Pap-Pap died outside?"

"Why is wonderful to die outside?" Anthony said, half-repeating the question, his mind miles away with his grief-stricken mother and sisters.

"Because," Stephanie said sweepingly, "he did not leave a hole in the roof when he went up to heaven!"

It was something to think about. In spite of our sadness, we basked in the simplicity and innocent wisdom of our small daughter and were comforted.

Pennsylvania was difficult, but because of Pap-Pap's goodness, it was bearable. He was, after all, just a little ahead of the rest of us.

Ultimately, we were glad that he had been taken home so painlessly, when so many others are not given that blessing. But it was Stephanie, who would one day grow up to be an accomplished actress, who recognized the high drama inherent in the untimely death of our beloved Pap-Pap.

Perhaps Pap-Pap was already influencing the angels in the beyond, because, on our return to Indiana, Anthony was asked to tutor a class in Western Civilization three evenings a week at Notre Dame. Our "janitor" was expanding his line of work, while his wife, resident of Fertile Valley, was just plain expanding!

Meanwhile . . . back in the hospital . . . I had a new baby. This time it was a little girl and we named her Mary Kay after her daddy's grandmother. Now we had three tow-heads, even though my genetics course in college had taught me to expect children with dark hair, because their father had such dominant-gened black hair.

Whenever Anthony was seized by a melodramatic urge, I was referred to as "a young mother, twice" but now the card that accompanied the red roses read: "To a young mother, thrice!"

Just lying there with the scent of roses in the air and with time for Anthony and me to get sufficiently acquainted with our daughter was delightful. Hospital stays, however, also offer time to do some serious thinking. Why couldn't I think of something no-one else had ever thought about to earn some money?

Propped up in the hospital bed, I began to employ everything I had read about concerning the processes of creative thinking and said to Anthony, "That is a pitcher of water, but is that the way a pitcher has to be? That is a window shade. How can a window shade be improved? Does it have to look and act in that fashion?"

"What do you expect to prove by all this?" Anthony asked.

"I'm going to invent something," I replied.

"Like what?" he insisted.

"I don't know yet. Something. Just anything."

"Well, go right ahead. But see that it doesn't cost me anything," he admonished, and then he smiled bravely.

Anthony had been in fairly good spirits about money lately because he had been awarded a Rockefeller Foundation fellowship to help him along with his graduate studies. The grant was the usual sum allocated to such fellowships, but this one, with the name "Rockefeller" attached to it, had a certain extra something to it. Psychologically, John D.'s money had a rubbery consistency. Somehow, one hundred dollars of his money went much farther than a similar amount from the janitorial job. Playing his Rockefeller role to the hilt, Anthony would thrust his lower lip and upper chest out at the same time, hand me the household money, pound the table with a heavy fist, and stoutly declare, "There you are, my good woman. And, remember, there's plenty more where this came from!"

Truer words were never spoken, to be sure, and window shades seemed to have been brought into existence for the express purpose of going up and down. But, by the time the mid-day nurse came in, there was another use for them!

A window shade, or just plain roll-up charts, could be painted with appropriate scenes and could transform any room in the house into a playhouse for a little girl. Why, with enough appropriate charts, an old attic could be developed into a make-believe gingerbread house!

"We could have a certain number of "roll-ups" for the kitchen, some for the bathroom. We could even develop charts of "weather windows" for the playhouse," I told Anthony, "and that way the painted-on windows could show spring, summer, autumn, or winter!"

"Oh, to be a little girl in America today," Anthony sighed wistfully.

"That's just it," I said. "I read an article the other day that said there aren't nearly as many toy ideas for little girls as there are for little boys. If you're going to invent something, it said to come up with a girl-toy and you'll have a better chance."

When we brought the baby home from the hospital, Stephanie was thrilled with a baby sister and, in her manipulative way, she made Robbie pleased, too.

Robbie had ordered a baby brother and he had also requested a Boy Scout canteen so that he could carry water and not have to stop in the middle of play to come home to get a drink. So, we bought him a canteen.

"See, Robbie," Stephanie pointed out to him magnanimously. "You got a canteen and I got a baby sister!" and Robbie nodded his complete satisfaction.

Meanwhile, I was still thinking of inventing a new kind of toy, girl-toys, boy-toys, neuter-gendered toys. But it was evident that Anthony was thinking about Charles II's preponderance on the Continent or else knee-deep again in Iconoclasm in the Latter Byzantine Empire. However, when the

Change-O-Clothes Doll was born, he became violently interested.

"What can you do with dolls but dress them with clothes and then take the clothes off again," I complained.

"I thought there were some dolls talented enough to have a wet diaper now and then," he said, looking up from his newspaper.

"Think of how unique it would be to just press a button, and, presto — the doll has a change of clothes!" Seeing the need for further explanation I said, "My doll would be divided into three parts, three clothes parts that is. There would be a hat, a blouse, and a skirt. The doll would be encased in celluloid or something. The different colors and patterns for its clothes would be painted on three long tapes. The little girl presses the button and all three tapes move — the one for the hat, the one for the blouse, and the one for the skirt. When they come to a halt, the little girl could see how her doll is dressed! She could amuse herself all day long trying to get the doll's clothes all matched up — the same color of hat, blouse, and skirt, or the same design. She'd keep trying and trying!" I paused for Anthony's approval, but Dr. Jekyl had suddenly become Mr. Hyde and Heathcliff rose from his chair and started toward me.

"You, — you one-armed bandit, you!" he roared. "Three lemons, three bells, — try for three bunches of cherries, or for the same kind of hat, blouse, and skirt!" he fumed. "What difference is there? A refined slot-machine, — that's what you'd have the little girls of America playing with!"

After five minutes more I had the basic rules of gambling under my cranium.

"So you see, little one," the professor was saying to his slow pupil, stroking her hair ever-so-gently, and ever-so-toleratingly, "a Change-O-Clothes Doll must never be. Little girls will learn soon enough about lemons, bells, and bunches of cherries. And it just wouldn't be right for them to learn it from a doll, now, would it?" I buried the Change-O-Clothes Doll idea, and life went on. But someone had to think of something for little girls to play with, and besides, I was earning my Ph.T., or was I?

And so, days later, I built a House-Of-Bread. The bread-house toy kit would contain some little racks into which ordinary slices of bread could be slipped, to form the walls of the house. There would be a structure for the roof, onto which two slices could be placed, forming a kind of slanting roof, and a window-cutter for bread slices that could lend themselves to being windows as well as walls, and there would even be little flower boxes to be placed beneath the cut-out windows. When a child finished his or her house of bread, he or she could paint it with jelly, butter, or even peanut butter and eat it!

However, when the bread roof caved in five times in succession, I decided to abandon inventing for children and enter the adult field of dreamed-up-gadgets.

A bed for pregnant women was the most sensible, practical thing I could come up with.

I decided to test it out on Anthony by saying, "Think of how many uncomfortable expectant mothers there are all over the country at this very moment. There are women who never get to sleep at night unless they lie on their stomachs, and how can you lie on your stomach when you're pregnant?"

"I wouldn't know," Anthony said flatly.

"Now, my bed would have an adjustable hole on one side, so that she could sleep on her tummy without any pressure on the baby!"

"What happens when she wants to lie on her back?" Anthony asked.

"That's what the other side of the bed is for. There's only one hole in the mattress, say, on the left. Then, the regular straight part is on the right."

Anthony was truly concerned as he asked, "Where is the husband?"

"He's in the old bed, the one they used before they bought the 'expectant mother's answer-to-a-prayer-bed'!"

"All they'd have to have is a twenty-four foot by twenty-eight foot bedroom," Anthony muttered, exasperated.

Finally, I had an idea worthy of a visit to a patent attorney's office. The idea was called "locked socks."

"I think you really have something this time," Anthony encouraged. The only thing that changed a regular pair of socks to the locked socks variety was an ordinary snap fastener. On one of the anklets was sewn the male end of the snap and on the other anklet, the female end. When the socks were taken off at night, they could be snapped together and put in the hamper. When they were thrown into the washer and dryer, they stayed locked together. They could even be hung on the clothesline together. The menial job of mating socks was over, for locked socks could be put, as is, in the drawer ready to be unlocked and worn. It was a truly practical idea.

"Just think," Anthony mused. "If sock manufacturers adopt your little idea I won't ever have to worry again about having the electricity turned off. You — you Edison you!" and he chucked me under the chin.

Wally, a former neighbor, was now a patent attorney, so, "See Wally" was at the top of my memo pad.

Wonder of wonders, Wally was optimistic! "Sounds good," he said. "It was practical. Everyone wears socks and it has wide appeal!"

So as Wally began his patent search, Anthony and I went home to look after the children and to study up on inheritance tax laws for them, confident that we had come up with a million dollar idea.

Three weeks later, a long, fat letter from Wally ended the suspense. The patent search was complete. Contained therein were clippings and various proofs that a Frenchman, whose name I chose to forget immediately, had beaten me to the draw by a margin of four months.

There, on that skimpy piece of paper, went my new dress, the down-payment on a house, educations for the children and a million other dreams.

"Cheer up," Anthony consoled. "You'll think of something else."

But his words were as sounding brass and tinkling cymbal. For a long time I could see nothing but the hole in the doughnut.

Robbie, Anthony, Stephanie, Virginia and Mary Kay in front of Black Manor shortly after moving in.

IV
Black Manor

Suddenly, through the darkness and out of the blue came wonderful news. Studebaker was hiring again! The engineering courses Anthony had had in the V-12 program for the U.S. Navy at Penn State were about to pay off! Testers of jet engines were needed. Men with engineering backgrounds were being recruited. In addition to a technical knowledge, strong eardrums that could take prolonged noises were a prerequisite.

So, the future professor went back to the factory again, for his family, for his country, and indirectly, for his Ph.D. A transfusion of good, rich, economic blood was now pumped into the Black family coffers, coffers that had been disastrously depleted.

Understandably, being on the night-shift at Studebaker and the day-shift at Notre Dame were bound to take a heavy toll on strength, nerves, and academia. The struggle to maintain scholarship on little sleep was a difficult one. The running of a home, even one as tiny as our Vetville home, with only one spouse in evidence most of the time, was rough. But with three children and only two bedrooms, it was apparent that a housing shortage was staring us in the face. Should we begin to look for new quarters? Had we outgrown our beloved Vetville?

Spurred on by the fat Studebaker paycheck, Anthony and I began to look for a house to fill our needs. The quest was on. Once a week, sandwiched between Sunday Mass and Mary Kay's afternoon nap, we went house hunting. One bright sunny day we spotted a big, old, white clapboarded, friendly-looking house that would be our "Home in Indiana" for the next six years.

"Black Manor," as we dubbed it, was only about a mile from Vetville and was situated on Angela Boulevard, very near to the entrance of Notre Dame. It was an ideal family home with five bedrooms, two baths, and lilac bushes along a white picket fence in the back. The price was a fair one, and in addition, there was one large cherry tree behind the house, an ample garage, and a coal furnace! Then, too, there was evidence that the neighbors to the north would be on the quiet side, they being the residents of Cedar Grove cemetery. By borrowing the down payment, juggling expenditures, and praying that the Studebaker government contracts would hold for a while longer, we prepared for the big move.

"Remember, Virginia," Anthony kept cautioning, "we're only going one skinny mile so this will be a very simple move."

I can still hear my mother's reasoning voice as she tried to explain moving procedures to the Ph.D. candidate: "Everything has to be packed regardless — whether you're going one mile or one thousand miles," she said over and over, but

Anthony remained unconvinced. To him Mother and I were making much ado about nothing, a skyscraper out of a matchbox or somesuch. The future professor's theory on moving reached its apex, however, when the moving of the refrigerator was contemplated.

"It's ridiculous to take anything out of the refrigerator," Anthony said. "We're going such a short distance. Just leave everything as is."

"Don't argue with him," I said quietly to his mother-in-law. "He'll get his come-uppance on moving day." And we went off to packing boxes, leaving the refrigerator untouched.

And soon, a "house-cooling" for the Vetville apartment was executed. Scores of paper icicles were attached to the boxes that Mother and I managed to fill, in spite of Anthony, and with flowing wine and pungent cheeses, we bid adieu to Vetville, our home for the last four and one half years. It was nice not to have to say good-bye to our Vetville friends, since, as Anthony would not let us forget, "We were really still in the area."

Moving day came in mid-March. The huge U-Haul waited outside on Hesburgh Way, and the boxes, one by one, along with things that were unboxable — lamp shades, bed-posts, mattresses and springs, tables, chairs, and chests of drawers — were loaded onto the truck. However, when the time came for the refrigerator, the air was charged with electric anticipation on the part of Mother and me.

The man with the dolly said, "I'll get the fridge!"

Anthony said, "I'll help you." Mother and I gathered in silence to watch.

The mover, with one great heave, hoisted the huge refrigerator onto the dolly. As he prepared to wheel the huge box out to the truck, he grabbed onto the handles of the dolly and with his right foot pushed forward. The inevitable came. As he pulled the whole "holy load" over to himself with one gargantuan grunt, Niagara went over the brink!

The shattering of pickle jars bumping into cauliflower left-overs, glass milk bottles colliding with ketchup dispensers, mustard jars smashing into egg cartons, and jellies scrunching into mashed-potato heaps filled the bristling air! The horrified look of consternation on the mover's face had an unusual accompaniment, as seconds later, the bottles and jars emptied themselves of their contents, dripping and trickling and gurgling all together.

In a muffled tone, Anthony said, "I guess we had best take everything out of the refrigerator before we go any farther." Mother bit her tongue and shook her head in wonderment, while I rushed to the innards of the clothes closet laughing surreptitiously at the sheer nonsense of it all.

Eventually moving day ended in the collapse of weary bodies. And in a matter of weeks, after the "settling in" had taken place, it seemed as though we had always occupied Black Manor.

The children reveled in the spaciousness of the Manor. Each child had his or her own bedroom. At least they did for a few hours until the newness closed in, and then it started: "I'm lonely in here, Mommy, Can't we sleep like we used to? Come hold my hand, Daddy. This room's too big!"

Black Manor's bigness had many advantages. There

was a room to be made into a study, and a large basement for all the cavalry sets, knights and ladies, puppet theaters, Chatty Cathy's, Lincoln Logs, tiddley-winks, erector sets, Snoopy dogs, doll houses, doll beds, Slinky coils, Show-boats, magic sets, Play-Dough Factories, Little Red Cabooses, skates, wagons, skooters, tricycles, xylophones, and drums.

The house was absolutely splendid! Notre Dame was within walking distance and even the supermarket was handy. In spite of the fact that Anthony had read a statistic that only 16 percent of the husbands in America do the weekly shopping for groceries, he continued to bring home the bacon in between his hectic schedule of testing jet engines and attending the graduate school at the University.

Putting away "what Daddy brought" was always an exciting time with little heads peering into the brown paper bags for a look at a new cereal offering or, perhaps, a lollipop or two. Yes, life at Black Manor was eventful. And having all this room was super. "Could we capitalize on it?" I wondered.

The moment the inspiration came to rent out two of our five bedrooms to Notre Dame students, I thought to myself, "I grew up to be a landlady!"

Hallelujah! I had a good, practical idea to raise money and Anthony cheered, "That's a great idea. We can stop worrying about meeting mortgage payments. The rent the students pay us will help pay the bank."

But, then I wondered, "What does a landlady do?" The only landladies I ever saw were the ones in the movies. These characters walked through the scene carrying a mop and pail with sweat on their foreheads and wisps of hair hanging down their necks. Their palms were always outstretched as they said, "Either ya pay up — or ya get out.'"

I somehow felt that I did not quite fit into this picture of a landlady, but I guess no landlady does. A woman friend, a widow, who had rented rooms to students for a number of years gave us sound advice: "They're not to cook in their rooms, and when they start flushing the lettuce leaves down the toilet, you're in for trouble."

Another friend, a man who had rented a room for a time in a distant city, gave me the viewpoint of the roomer: "Tell you what I always did," he confided. "I would test the landlady out the first few days. I'd hedge on things, just to see how much she was willing to do. For instance, I'd leave a few things like a pair of pants, a coat, etc., scattered around the room. If she hung them up, then I would expect it the year round. But if she walked around the mess, then I'd know that I had better do it. It's a battle of wits, ya might say."

With three small children and the house to take care of, I was hoping my roomers wouldn't be too careless. On the other hand, I was hoping that the students would adjust to the noisy prattle of my offspring.

The leaves started to fall as the middle of September came, and with it, my students — three handsome boys, ages 21, 20, and 19, with bag and baggage. The double room went to brothers, Jerry

and Jack, who were from Minnesota. The single room
went to Mike, a widow's son from Illinois.

All three were commerce majors, a junior and two
sophomores. When they completed their training,
they would be able to handle responsible jobs in
the business world, but right now they were only
interested in whether or not they had ample closet
space and what time they were to be in at night.
They readily discovered that the light in one
bedroom was a temperamental thing, that it
required a little coaxing to stay lit, that the
window in their bathroom could not be raised
because it had been painted shut, and that when
their showers were of a longer-than-usual
duration, little trickles of water would find
their way into the kitchen downstairs.

All three of the boys had been exposed to
dormitory living. But none had been exposed to a
home that counted six active little feet.

"You're not to go into the students' rooms. They
must study," became my battle-cry.

"But I made a present for them," the five-year-
old would say, holding up the work of his fingers,
a crude little crayoned house or a clay-wrought
apple or banana.

Six-year-old Stephanie would petition, "Can I
take some popcorn to them? I know they're hungry."

The deep, masculine voices that suddenly filled
the house made it seem as though we were having a
prolonged stag party, and that the guests were
enjoying themselves so much that they weren't
going to go home, ever. But this was their home!
My husband and I had whirl-windishly acquired
three grown sons!

The telephone would ring: "Is Jack there?" the voice would ask. The inventory was now: Anthony, Virginia, Stephanie, Robbie, Mary Kay, Jerry, Mike and Jack. So, it took a minute to respond at first, as I mentally adjusted to my expanded family.

When I discovered that my men, my "roomers," were daily making their own beds, I protested, "You don't have to do that. Landladies expect to make the beds."

"We have no sisters," the brothers explained, "and we're used to doing it at home and besides," they added a little sheepishly, "we had orders before we left home!"

My difficult task was keeping Mary Kay from discovering their alarm clocks. Once she started walking she extracted a chortling delight from throwing the students' clocks down the stairs!

On the eve of the feast of St. Nicholas, December 6, there were not only three tiny pairs of shoes placed out on the front porch, to await St. Nick's generosity, but three man-sized pairs of brown oxfords as well.

"You'll see," Stephanie assured the students. "St. Nicholas will leave you something." And they were not disappointed. The next morning they cheerfully went off to their classes sucking contentedly on large peppermint sticks.

In February, Jack was notified that there was room for him on the campus of Notre Dame, the aim of the University being that all underclassmen should live within the shadow of the Golden Dome. When this happened, Mike abandoned his private room and moved in with Jerry, while I advertised

in student publications that a student room was
available.

It was in the deepest of the deep snows that a
knock came to the door, and with it, a request to
see the vacant room. He was a graduate student in
sociology. He was tall, neatly dressed, and
polite. He liked the room and said he'd like to
take it immediately.

"But why do you want the room now?" I asked. "I
thought everyone was settled since the semester
began weeks ago."

"Because," he said slowly, and very quietly, "my
landlady dropped dead this morning and the heirs
have already informed us that they have other
plans for the house."

"Oh," was the only reply I could muster.

A few days after Randolph, that was his name,
was settled in his new quarters, I was curious to
know more about the landlady whose career had
ended so abruptly. "Tell me," I began, "had she
been ill?"

"No, not at all," Randolph answered, pausing a
moment on his way out the side door. "My landlady
and I had been talking in the kitchen. The other
students were out. She was sitting at the table
and I was standing in the doorway, when all of a
sudden, she just fell over. I applied artificial
respiration and called a doctor, but it was no
use. She was about eighty-eight years of age."

Before I could question him further, he
mentioned that he was already late for class.

"The poor woman," I commented to my husband
later. "And imagine what a harrowing experience it
was for Randolph." I thought to myself, "I

certainly would like to know what they were
talking about when she keeled over." That evening,
when Randolph came downstairs to inquire about
linen provisions, I had my chance.

"Tell me," I said, as I leaned over somewhat in
anticipation of the momentous answer I expected.
"What were you and your landlady talking about
when — when it happened?" And then I added
solemnly, "What were her last words?"

"Well," Randolph said, smoothing down his hair
somewhat, "we were just having a quiet chat. She
had commented on what she was planning to have for
lunch . . . ."

"Yes?" I was on the edge of my chair in
expectation.

Melodramatically, Randolph continued: "Her last
words were: 'I think I'll have a jelly sandwich
and some of that leftover vegetable soup.' That
was it!"

"That's all?" I found myself incredulous.

"For Moses' sake!" Anthony broke in, "What did
you want her to say?"

"I don't know . . .," I answered, concentrating
on my own thoughts. "It's too bad, though, that
her last words had to be about leftovers. Don't
you agree?"

A few days later, after I had reiterated the
landlady's sudden exit from this world to a
friend, she consoled me with the knowledge that
she was certain that had the poor woman known that
these would be her last words she certainly would
have said something else!

But I was certain of only one thing. If my new
roomer, namely Randolph, ever asked me what I was

planning to have for lunch and my menu consisted of a jelly sandwich and some left-over vegetable soup, I'd be darn sure to keep it to myself.

Life at Black Manor went on and soon the snow had melted and it was spring again. The crocuses, tulips, and daffodils pushed above the ground and along with summer came students smearing on sun tan lotion, driving to nearby lakes, and having their girls "down" for the prom.

The school year came to a literal bang-up close when the brakes on Mike's car locked, and he hit a police car.

With the school year over and the students home for summer vacation, there was nothing left for a landlady to do but air the beds, send the drapes to the cleaners, and stretch the budget until student roomers, once again, made their appearance.

*   *   *   *

One late summer evening, while reading the SOUTH BEND TRIBUNE, another solution to our budget problems leaped off the page. It read:

"Rooms needed at once, for the football crowd. Call the South Bend Chamber of Commerce if you have an extra sleeping room. Local hotels, motels full to capacity. Give us your name, address, rent wanted. You'll be glad you did!"

Well now, here we were, the fourth closest house to the Notre Dame football stadium and although every extra bedroom in the house was already rented to Notre Dame students, I knew there had to

be a way to squeeze in a few more people for a
weekend.

There was no time to waste. I had speculated for
weeks and now in just four days, thousands of
Oklahomans with their tall hats and fat oil money
would invade our fair city! I knew I had to talk
it over with Anthony when he got home and then
call the Chamber of Commerce first thing in the
morning.

That evening, however, I didn't have the
opportunity to discuss a subject as sensitive as
this, so I left it for the morning. But just as I
was about to tell him of my brilliant idea, he
dashed out of the house for his eight o'clock
class. Little did he know he was about to play a
role in solving South Bend's football housing
problem.

I knew I would have to act fast, because time
was of the essence. I told myself, "He won't mind
my not consulting him just this once."

So I called the Chamber of Commerce and when a
lady answered the phone, I told her I was
inquiring about the ad.

The first thing she asked was, "What kind of
room it it?"

"Well, it's blue . . .," I muttered.

"Is it a single or double?" she patiently
continued, requesting specific information.

"There's a double bed in it," I persisted.

"You may charge anything from four dollars to
twelve dollars a night," she further intoned,
"whatever you think is fair. The price depends on
the condition of the room and the location of your
home. We'll call you as soon as we have someone
for you."

So it was done. "What should I charge?" I wondered. My mind zoomed up to the ceiling of twelve dollars and then thumped down to rock bottom, four dollars a night. Up, down. Down, up. But actually, what to charge was not the real problem at the moment. The cold, hard fact was that perfect strangers would soon occupy our own four poster bed and I hadn't let my husband know that I had literally rented our bed right out from under him.

There was no time to think of consequences. There was our room to clean, drawers to empty, a closet to clear. I would have to ask one of the students to lend an easy chair, and as Mike was the first one home I asked him.

"Mike," I called from the kitchen, "would you do me a favor?"

"Sure thing," he said congenially, as his head came around the frame of the doorway. "What is it?"

"I'm renting out Mr. Black's and my bedroom over the weekend to football fans and I was wondering if I could use the easy chair in your room for a day or so."

"Sure," Mike agreed. "But you can't sleep in a chair all night. I'll sleep in it."

"No, you don't understand," I explained. "No one will sleep in it; it's for the football people just to sit down in. Mr. Black and I will sleep downstairs on the sofa-bed in the living room. The couch opens up . . . ."

The baby was still napping, so I set about dusting the whiskers off the bedroom ceiling, vacuuming, and making room for my paying guests. Then the phone rang!

"Mr. and Mrs. Stevenson from Tulsa, Oklahoma," my lady friend from the Chamber of Commerce reported, "wish to speak to you about a room."

"Already?" I was aghast. "Yes, put them on."

"Hello," said an unfamiliar feminine voice. "We've just arrived!"

"Welcome to South Bend," I answered.

"I understand you have a room to rent. Is it a double?" the voice continued in a border-line, suspicious tone.

"It has a double bed in it," I nervously described, "and a chest of drawers, a dresser, an easy chair . . . ."

"I'm sure it will be fine," the woman from Oklahoma assured me, as beams of sunshine came out my end of the phone. "We'll be there in half an hour," she said — the boom fell!

"Fine," I managed weakly. "I'll be expecting you." I hung up the receiver with one hand and grabbed the dust mop with the other. There was still dusting to do and the chair to move! And Mike had gone out again!

I pulled the clothes out of one drawer and then stashed them into another, while baby Mary Kay, up now and wide-awake, confused the procedure with methods of her own.

Now to get the man-sized chair through my lady-like door frame. This was not to be accomplished in minutes. I succeeded in unburdening Mike's room of the chair, wrestled with it in the hallway and finally got it partially through the bedroom doorway when the doorbell rang.

"They're here! And what a mess I am," I cried as I caught a glimpse of myself in the upstairs hall mirror.

To think that one thin door could separate such a contrast. Mrs. Stevenson was chic, attractively dressed, tall, dark, and well-jewelled! And here I was: short, tousled, dishevelledly arranged, and with safety-pins mounted on my bosom!

We exchanged greetings.

Mrs. Stevenson was charming and a whole halo of Oklahoma sunshine framed her head. Mr. Stevenson was a handsome fortyish with hair, dignity, and a good crease to his trousers.

I thought to myself, "That will be ten dollars a night for the room."

"I was wondering," Mr. Stevenson said, breaking into my innermost thoughts, "would you happen to have a garage where I could put my car?"

"Certainly," I accommodated, "You can use the garage in the rear. Our car is only a '51, and we seldom put it away."

"Well," Mr. Stevenson drawled, "my car is only a '47, but I'd prefer to keep it in a garage."

I said to myself, "That will be four dollars a night, and the soap and towels are free."

"I'll show you the room," I said aloud, and together, the Stevensons, baby Mary Kay, and myself, mounted the stairs. As we approached, there was the maroon-covered easy chair, where I had left it, stuck in the doorway!

"Everything is ready except for this chair," I apologized. "I guess I need a little help to get it through." Mr. Stevenson sized up the situation immediately. He carefully placed his Oshkosh in a suitable spot on the rug, took off his gray flannel jacket, and magnanimously heaved the great chair through the door.

"Now," he asked, "where does it go?"

"Steve is handy at home, too," Mrs. Stevenson was saying.

I thanked him heartily and then gestured: "Here are your towels and soap. There's drawer space here, and . . . ."

"When do we pay?" Mrs. Stevenson wanted to know.

"This is just like a hotel," I said in my best business voice, "when you leave."

With that, Mary Kay and I made our exit so the Stevensons could relax a bit and shake some of the Oklahoma clay from their shoes.

"A '47 car and he moved the chair to boot," I said to myself, "I'll charge them only five dollars. Of course the car could be a classic, maybe seven dollars."

When Stephanie and Robbie appeared from their play, they found it difficult to accept the fact that neither Uncle nor Aunt nor friends were living with us temporarily.

Robbie socked it to me, "They're strangers, aren't they?"

"But I hope they'll feel at home anyway," Stephanie commented.

Later that evening, Mrs. Stevenson politely asked, "Would you mind very much if we dried a few things in your dryer?"

"Not at all," I truthfully answered. "I want you to make yourselves at home." By six o'clock that evening, I was convinced that the Stevensons had taken me at my word. In just those few short hours, Mrs. Stevenson had changed Mary Kay's diapers twice, informed me of the oil refining business in Oklahoma, and transplanted a clump of peony stalks that had blocked their car's entrance to the garage. Mr. Stevenson, with the help of one lone screw-driver, fixed the handle on the rake, tightened every door knob in the house, and was adroitly adjusting the television when Anthony appeared on the scene!

"We have company!" I beamed at Anthony, offering the skimpiest of introductions, as I quickly hurried him into the linen closet for a brief consultation.

"Sure, it's okay," he whispered. "I can stand anything for one night."

Four nights later, however, Anthony's enthusiasm was as sheer as one of Salome's veils. "When are the Stevensons going home?" he wanted to know. "The football game's been over for quite some time. They're fine people and all that, but I'm tired of sleeping down here and having to explain them to everybody."

Departure time finally came and the Stevensons said, "Well, what do we owe you? Tell us now, because we'll be gone before you wake up in the morning."

When I replied I didn't know what to charge, they said that the woman at the Chamber of Commerce thought it would be around ten dollars per night.

"Let's make it seven dollars a night," I stammered, thinking of our unpaid bills, and yet, remembering all the Stevensons' services to us.

"Fine," Mr. Stevenson agreed with a wide grin, and reached for his billfold.

Meanwhile, Stephanie, witnessing the entire transaction, was genuinely horrified! "Mother!"

she cried. "You're not charging these nice people money because they stayed with us, are you?"

Totally embarrassed and not knowing what to say, Mr. Stevenson came to my rescue with a brave attempt to explain the basic facts of supply and demand and elementary economics to Stephanie, but to no avail. He then paid his bill and made reservations for the following year when Notre Dame would again play the mighty Sooners.

Once the football season had ended, I thought the opportunity for making extra money by renting out our bedroom had also ended, but it was apparent that my reputation as a kindly landlady was spreading, for here at my front door stood two white-buck-shoed Notre Dame students with a request that was to help our budget tremendously.

"Mrs. Black," the one boy said, "a friend of ours told us that you might have a room you could rent to our girl-friends for the weekend of the big dance, and we thought it would help to be so close and everything . . . ."

"Yeah," chimed in the other, "no cabs back and forth from a hotel in town — we don't have a car, you know."

I immediately replied, "Sure, I'll have a room for them. When will they be here?"

"In another month," the dark-haired one replied. "We came in plenty of time to be sure of the arrangement."

"Call me a day or so before the dance," I requested, "to let me know the exact time they'll be here. I want everything to be just right."

Breaking the news to Anthony was the difficult part of the enterprise.

"And just what room do we have available for a weekend?" Anthony asked.

"Our bedroom, again, of course. If Notre Dame holds enough dances, we might even be able to muster up the taxes on the house."

There was no reply as the Lord of the Manor returned to the Napoleonic Wars.

When the girls did arrive, Black Manor "Motel" took on a strange new appearance. The odors of pungent, exotic perfumes filled the hallways as high-heeled shoes on delicately formed feet clicked upstairs, downstairs, in and out. Silk stockings were draped gracefully and ungracefully in the bathroom, while crinoline slips that refused to be confined to closets stuck out of doors like taffy candy gone astray.

I thought our boys, "regular renters" from Notre Dame, would be delighted to have pretty girls staying in our bedroom for Notre Dame dances, but that was not the original response. In fact, our regular roomer Jerry made the comment, "Your children are quiet compared to those chatterboxes," while Mike voiced his objection by saying, "Do you suppose I could make an appointment to get into the bathroom?"

Later from his spot on the sofa-bed Anthony said, "The only thing I'm hoping for is that they are careful not to spill any of those sickeningly sweet colognes on our bed, at least not on my side."

I assured him, "Oh, they'll be careful." And soon the majority of those inhabiting Black Manor were asleep.

The girls came and went as Notre Dame dances

proceeded through the school year. But an unforeseen complication cropped up at Mardi Gras time which marred the heretofore successful endeavor.

The annual Mardi Gras dance was a Notre Dame tradition and I had promised some students, weeks ahead of time, that I would have room for their girl friends.

And how these two particular girls came! In a great swish of hat-boxes, luminous-luggage, giggles, and click-clacking transparent heels. "This is wonderful!" they cried appreciatively. "It's such a lovely room. And to be so close to the University! And the boys! Now, are you sure we're not putting you out?"

"Not at all, not at all," I reassured them as I mentally counted my budget for the month. I went downstairs and left them to their curlers and creams.

"Did the girls get here all right?" Anthony inquired when he got home at dinner-time.

"Yes," I replied, "can't you smell them?"

"Not above the cabbage you're cooking," he replied, as the sauerkraut sputtered and gurgled in the background.

"I see we have more company," Jerry and Mike said through gritted teeth. "How long will they be staying?"

I assured them that they'd stay just through Saturday night and be gone by early Sunday afternoon. "And boys," I added, "since you'll be going to the dance yourselves tonight, I'll leave the side door open. Mr. Black and I will be sleeping on the sofa-bed in the living room so avoid the front door."

"Okay," they mumbled as they rushed to retake possession of the bathroom.

At nine that evening, one after the other, each resplendent in his or her own particular dance attire, descended the stairs. First, "our boys" in tuxedos and bow ties, and then the girls as their young men arrived on the scene.

Even Stephanie had stayed up to watch the procession. "Oh," she gasped at the gossamer dresses, "you both look exactly like Cinderella."

The girls laughed and one of them said, "Going to, or coming from?"

I truthfully told them, "You look positively beautiful."

And they went out into the night air to the Mardi Gras on the arms of their attentive beaux.

"To bed, Stephanie," I ordered, and she, too, disappeared.

"Here's part of the paper," Anthony said. "Care to read it?"

I yawned and replied, "For a few minutes, I'm pretty tired. I want to go to bed early."

Fifteen minutes later, a peculiar-looking, brow-twisting Anthony glanced over at me from his chair in the living room and said, "What did you say you planned on doing tonight?"

"I'm going to bed," I answered, failing to see his point.

"On what?" was all he said.

The walls of Jericho fell on me as I, too, discerned the truth! The sofa-bed had been sent to the factory weeks ago because of a structural defect and the company had sent an ordinary sofa to be used in its absence. We didn't have our comfortable, open-out hide-a-bed.

"Good heavens! It's ten o'clock already! What do we do now?"

Anthony joked and said, "I could go to the YMCA, but what about you? Someone has to stay with the children! Of course, we could talk to Jerry and Mike when they get home and get them to rent their room to us for the night . . . ."

"Be serious," I exploded. "What are we going to do?" One of us could sleep on the sofa, that was certain. But the floor loomed hard before us. There was still a light on at my neighbor's. Frances would help. She always did. I dialed quickly.

"Frances," I began, "I could tell you a lie and say that we just got some unexpected company, but I'll tell you the truth." In the next few minutes she had the story, and also a confession of complete stupidity — how two supposedly sane adults could overlook such a fundamental basic fact . . . .

"But, Virginia," she offered, "the only thing I can give you is one of those inflatable Boy-Scout mattresses. You know, the kind you have to blow up!" "Fine," I said, "anything will be better than the floor."

A few minutes later, Anthony returned with all the equipment, the inflatable pillow, air pump, and the khaki-colored balloon of a mattress!

My, but we worked so hard to get to bed! "One, two, three, — hip," we alternated blowing and pumping. Finally, we fell exhausted into our make-shift bed, a rubber raft in the middle of an ocean of broadloom. And sleep, the gentle thing, came, but not for long.

Out of the darkness a deep voice said, "But, I do love you."

To which a sweet voice replied, "Why didn't you dance number eight with me if you love me?"

The dance. Of course! One of the girls was home from the dance, and she and her boyfriend had no idea that we were lying on the floor almost underneath their feet.

I gave Anthony a poke to wake him up.

"What do you think you're doing?" he roared groggily.

With that, the startled Romeo of the hour took a step in the wrong direction and tumbled, ker-plunk, into the middle of our rubbery bed. After some scuffling, apologies, hasty explanations, and so forth, Black Manor settled down for the night.

"We should have hung a light to mark us," I said. "No one expects anyone to be sleeping on the floor."

Anthony grumbled, "They wouldn't have seen it anyway. They're too much in love."

The next morning we picked up our bed and walked to the cellar with it. There was no sense in deflating it, as we had to sleep on it again Saturday night.

Soon Sunday came and with it departure time for the girls.

As I was preparing lunch the phone rang. "Mrs. Black," said the deep voice, "this is Buster. Remember me?"

I didn't.

"Well," he went on, "my girl stayed at your house for one of the dances and now she is in town again, but her room is way over on the other side

of town and she has to catch a train. And, well,
we were wondering, could she change her dress in
your bedroom, the room she stayed in before? It
would help us out a lot by saving time and cab
fare."

"Sure. Come ahead," I found myself saying. "I'll
be glad to help."

By two o'clock that afternoon, the nights I had
spent on the rubber mattress were beginning to
take effect. "I'm going up for a nap," I told
Anthony. "I'll go to one of the children's beds,
since that girl is coming to change her dress in
our room."

Afterwards, Anthony reported that all went well.
The children had behaved for him and the girl had
come, changed her dress, and gone on her way.
Everything was just about normal again.

Monday morning I began my usual cleaning
schedule. In our bedroom I found what I had
expected. Bobby pins on the floor, facial tissues
scattered hither and thither, and little feminine
trinkets and discarded ribbons. But when I moved
the bed out so that the sweeper could do its work,
there, on the floor, was the oddest-looking
contraption. It had metal prongs of some kind on
the one end with little prongs on the other, and a
long electric cord. "This looks like something for
the Smithsonian Institution," I said to myself,
confiscating the oddity.

"Maybe it's part of one of our student's
experiments from the business lab," Anthony joked.
"Nope. Not mine. Not ours," the students informed.

"Put it in the Lost and Found," Anthony
concluded. "Someone, someday, will claim it." I

did what he suggested and promptly forgot the whole matter.

A few weeks later, Anthony bravely suggested we should go to Sunday Mass as a family with baby Mary Kay in tow. and after church he told the children, "Because you behaved so well, I'm going to treat everyone to lunch at the Notre Dame cafeteria."

"Hooray!" they squealed.

Soon the Black family was all gathered around the table in the center section of the cafeteria. "This is wonderful," I said to Anthony. "No cooking, no mess, no dishes to wash . . . ." And there I sat, serene and at peace with my family and the world, when all of a sudden, a startlingly deep masculine voice came from behind.

"Mrs. Black? . . . yeah . . . remember me? Buster? Say, did you happen to find my girl's electric eyelash curler in your bedroom by any chance?"

*   *   *   *

The June sun was brilliantly bright. My ad, which stated that I had two lovely bedrooms ideal for college students, was posted on a bulletin board in the Administration Building of the University of Notre Dame. Summer school would be starting in a matter of days. It was time for the boys to get settled.

Before many hours passed there stood Albert, a rebel from the South, who was asking to live with us. He stood hesitantly in the front doorway that first evening, with the red summer sun serving as

a backdrop, with crutches under one arm and a
cymbal and small drum under the other. The
crutches were being used temporarily, he
explained, to help a minor foot injury. The drums?
Well, he wouldn't need to practice in his room. He
merely was a drummer for a dance band at home in
North Carolina and thought perhaps he might pick
up a few dollars at local dances if anyone was
ever in need of a drummer. He then heaved in a few
ordinary-looking suitcases, an assortment of
boxes, and several space mobiles. The final bit of
unpacking, however, was heralded by Robbie who ran
into the living room from the front porch
exclaiming:

"Jesus is coming! Jesus is coming!"

Albert and his helper-friend explained, under
the weight of a three and one half foot bust of a
bearded man, that "it" was not Brahms, that "it"
could or could not be Socrates, but that "it," the
head, had been picked up at an auction for only
five dollars and was indeed a treasure.

A second student, Franchito, a Mexican-American
math teacher from a Texas high school, also joined
us while he worked on his Master's degree in
education at Notre Dame. He had never been as far
north as Indiana and I feared that he might get
homesick. So the first night or so after his
arrival, I found myself cooking tacos to make
things at least smell a little more South-of-the-
Borderish.

The six weeks session progressed rapidly and,
before I had even learned to make tortillas, it
was all over. At the close of summer school
Franchito went back to Texas, Albert returned to

North Carolina, and I began anew my fall housecleaning. When I got to the former students' room, however, I found that it was still occupied!

Socrates, Plato, Brahms, whatever, — the head that Albert had brought with him when he first moved in was still with us. Since it was such a large, heavy bust, I was truly perturbed. I could move it only with difficulty, and it occupied at least three-fourths of the closet.

When week-end guests from Pennsylvania appeared, we placed the bust on a table in the guest room and acted as though it was a perfectly natural part of the furnishings. When their eyes took in the three-foot statue, they said either nothing or a complete mouthful. About this time, Anthony would whisper to them that it was an ancestor of mine and not to say anything that would hurt my feelings. Before the company left, however, they were told the truth and all would proffer guesses as to whose head it might be.

Then one day, while talking to a neighbor over the backyard fence, a bell sounded in my head:

"And," the neighbor was saying, "we heard students talking at a pep rally before the last Notre Dame game. They said that there is a woman on Angela Boulevard who has a statue of Father Sorin in her closet. They announced at the rally that Father Sorin couldn't make the game on Saturday because he had gone back to Le Mans, France, for a visit. But these students laughed and said that Sorin wasn't in France at all, that he was nearby in a woman's closet.

The wheels turned. I was a woman. I lived on Angela Boulevard. And I had somebody's head in my closet!

We invited a priest-friend to dinner to inspect "the head." On the way to the closet I told him, "I think it might be Brahms. But Anthony always insists it is Socrates." (Anthony and I decided to stick to our original thoughts and see if Father could come up with the answer.) "Whoever this is, he's got to go, because he's taking up entirely too much space." I then opened the closet.

"By God," he declared solemnly, "it's Father Sorin himself!"

"The founder of Notre Dame?" I exclaimed!

"The same!" Father responded, throwing back his head in a hearty laugh.

A phone call to the prefect of discipline's office set the record straight. Father Sorin had indeed been missing from his pedestal in the Administration Building for some time. Yes, he had been reported to be all around the world. In times past, a student prankster would send postcards to the Student Body supposedly from Father Sorin — from France, England, Japan, California, etc.

When an Oklahoma-Notre Dame game was in the offing, Father Sorin would invariably write from Oklahoma City saying, "Just looking things over. Be back in time for the rally." And then at a dramatic moment, with much fanfare, the student M.C. would announce Father Sorin's arrival, amid cheers and applause, and the spotlight would focus on the head! After the pep assembly the bust would be restored to its pedestal in the Administration Building, only to disappear again some future midnight.

"Sure," said the Prefect of Discipline. "I'll send two reliable boys over right away to bring Father home."

"Imagine that Albert duping me like that," I said to Anthony, "and to think that I really believed he bought the sculpture for five dollars at an auction."

To which Anthony replied, "Just think, in your future ads for rooms you can boast: 'Father Sorin slept here.'"

V
Primary Teachers Wear Halos

By the end of summer the Studebaker job was over and it was apparent once again that part-time jobs for men were non-existent. But there were a few jobs available for women. The papers kept saying, "The teacher shortage is acute." So I applied to School City of South Bend and was promptly hired. A dear friend agreed to care for the children.

Ten years before, I had graduated from Seton Hill College in Greensburg, Pennsylvania, prepared to teach English in a high school somewhere in Pennsylvania. But, alas, no high school somewhere in Pennsylvania needed a newly graduated English major, and so I taught not only grammar, but also health, geography, history, spelling, writing, arithmetic, and you-name-it, all on an "emergency" license to fifth and sixth grade students in Natrona, Pennsylvania.

With the help of a current "emergency" certificate I was given thirty-eight South Bend second-graders to teach, to train, to tackle!

"Get in your seats," I said sweetly the first day. Not a child moved. "Children . . .," my voice was lost in the din. The room was ascream with shouting and laughter. Boys were chasing one

another around the room. Boys were wrestling in
every corner. Boys were in heaps, everywhere. Even
the inanimate, the erasers, zoomed with great
speed through the air. Girls were stringing out
portions of bubble gum to see who could get the
longest stretch, and at least ten of both sexes
were around my desk shouting in unison:
"She took my pencil."
"He stole my eraser!"
"She put gum on me!"
"Look at Johnny!"
"When do we go home?"
"Will we have 'rithmetic?"
"Where did you say I should sit?"
"I lost my bus money."
"Will we have chocolate cookies with our milk?"
The second graders were here, there, and
everywhere, and they just kept going! But before
the week was over, I discovered that I could, and,
at a moment's notice, get order in my room. I had
only to act like a mad woman! With a ping pong
paddle in hand I marched down aisle after aisle
banging an occasional desk with a loud whack! The
surprise element was the only thing that worked.

I began the schoolyear in September with all
sorts of aesthetic theories of why small children
behave the way they do, but by June I found it
difficult to understand why primary teachers were
not an extinct species. The struggle for order in
the classroom was an omnipresent thing.

One little boy in the middle of the lesson would
leave his seat and sprawl out on the floor in a
comfortable position. After getting desperately
tired of telling him to get into his seat and

having no authority to whack him into it (a lawsuit was pending against a teacher in the community who had paddled a child), I consulted his mother. She, a lovely woman, told me that they had taken a long auto trip the previous summer and he had spent most of his time lying on the floor in the back seat of the car and that he liked to lie on floors. She smiled proudly at his "studied individuality" — as she labeled it.

Another child like to view me and the front of the classroom from an upside-down position. She would turn her chair around and place her head on the floor and look at life in the classroom from this particular angle.

Another child liked to crawl on the floor. At any given moment he would leave his seat and crawl up and down the aisle until he was noticed and made to sit down again.

When I complained to the principal, I was told that this was "normal behavior — seven-year-olds act like this all over the country."

"God help the country," I said to myself. Fortunately, I learned, he was a maverick principal.

One little girl with a pathetically low I.Q. insisted on tickling me every chance she had. She would attack me from behind, aiming for the area nearest my armpits. I scolded. I even tried to ignore the situation by pretending I was not the least bit ticklish, a difficult thing to do when the chills were chasing one another up and down my spine like an elevator out of control!

It was the tickling problem, however, that led me to seek help. "I think it is extremely odd behavior," I confided to the principal. "I'd like to discuss the matter with the school psychologist."

Mr. Principal pursed his lips a moment in deep thought and then said conclusively: "I think it is perfectly normal for a child to tickle his teacher."

I tried to analyze the mess I had gotten into. Where had I failed? I had two successful years as a teacher behind me. If this had been my first year, I would have truly considered myself a misfit and would have tried something like working at the local beanery.

But my fifth graders had behaved. I had loved those kids and they loved me. Could I have lost the touch during those years of keeping house and child bearing?

"I'll put every last one of you in the corner," I found myself shouting desperately at them the next day. When the room at last was quiet I sank into my chair at the desk, exhausted, defeated, and discouraged. As Sandy, a little blond, pig-tailed, blue-eyed second-grader was approaching the desk, I asked myself, "Now what?"

"Mrs. Black," she said, her large expressive eyes suddenly brimming with tears. "You're the poorest teacher I ever had!"

My heart stood still! This—this baby— truly felt my inadequacy! What tremendous insight! For a child! But what a blow to the ego. True, I was only the third teacher Sandy had ever had. There was kindergarten, first grade and then second. The poorest of the three!

"Yes," Sandy kept on, "you really are the

poorest. You don't have a television set or a fur coat — you're really the poorest teacher I ever had!"

I took her little hands in mine. "God's in His heaven, all's right with the world," I thought, counting my blessings.

The children were always talking about the HOWDY DOODY show on television. Invariably someone would ask me about it and I would say: "No, I'm sorry. We haven't bought a television set yet. I haven't seen the show. As for the fur coat, since no teacher wore a fur coat to school I can't imagine what prompted this in Sandy's mind, but when you got right down to it, things were mounting to an explosive climax via the so-called "reading circle."

The chore of sitting with the children on those tiny chairs, saying softly and sweetly, "All right now, sound it out . . .," was getting to me.

I hadn't the patience, the endurance, the grit, the temperament to survive. Day after day, lesson after lesson came the hideous sounds:

"K-k-k-k-k-k-k!

"S-s-s-s-s-s!

"D-d-d-d-d-d!" or "K-k-k-k A-a-a-a-a T-t-t-t-t!"

They came spasmodically. They came gutturally, nasally, and explosively. They came jerkily. You wanted to grab the kid, shake the sputterer, and say: "It's cat, damn you, cat!" But instead, you smiled, pulled in your intestines, and softly purred: "Now, what are the sounds saying, dear?"

And the agony continued:

"N-n-n-n-n-n, B-b-b-b-b-b, O-o-o-o-o-o-o!"

And then the advanced pupils:

"Look . . . Look at . . . Look at the ball!"

And:

"Look and see. See the ball. Oh, look, look, look! See the ball!"

Then, one sunny day, at a meeting the principal called primarily in order to decide whether or not the school would be permitted to use ball point pens for penmanship lessons, I learned that officials from neighboring township schools were coming to inspect our brand new, well-equipped, green blackboarded school.

"These men are out for ideas," the principal told us. "They are building or will soon build schools in their own areas and they want to see what we have. Make your rooms as attractive as you can. Be courteous to them and answer all their questions to the best of your ability. They won't visit every classroom, but if they happen into yours, take the time to be helpful. They will appreciate it."

A few days later the group of school board members arrived — butchers, bakers, and candlestick makers, the great American taxpayers, about to decide just what their particular schools needed in the line of furnishings.

My classroom was ready for them! The boards were their greenest green and the movable desks were moving as usual! The second-graders had even behaved long enough to paint lively night scenes on large sheets of art paper. Their dark, blue skies were in excellent contrast to their round yellow moons.

"But why," the supervising art teacher asked my class, "did you decide to paint night scenes?"

A little dark-haired moppet raised her hand and truthfully replied, "'Cause Mrs. Black told us to paint the night so that the dark sky should go with the light bricks on the walls of this room!" The truth was out!

The visiting school board members were not so easily answered. "Your children have to stand up in order to look out of the windows!" one said in shocked amazement. "Why is that? The school we are planning will have floor-length windows — like a living room at home. We feel that the school should be as much like the home as possible!" Having finished his soliloquy, he turned to me for approval.

In as polite a tone as I could muster, I pointed out to him that there were enough distractions in an ordinary classroom without gigantic windows to boot.

"Well, then," he said in a toleratingly challenging tone, "what sort of windows would you say would be ideal for your notion of a school?"

"Tiny peepholes in the ceiling," I said, looking him straight in the eye and pointing heavenward with an index finger.

"Well then," he said, arching his back. "I suppose you're not in favor of these movable desks either . . ." and he gestured deskward.

"No, I'm not. I'm for the nailed-down, old fashioned variety. And," I was gathering steam, "I feel that if I could chain a few of my pupils to their seats, forcing them to sit still for ten minutes at a time, they'd learn something in spite of themselves!" There, it was out!

"I see!" Mr. School-Board Member said in an all-

knowing tone. At this the second-graders reached
the crest of their noise crescendo and the
official bowed feebly through the door, mumbling
something as he went.

The school days continued to snail by, with my
throat getting rawer and my patience thinner, but
finally June did manage to arrive on schedule.

When the last report card had been given out and
the last scream of a pupil echoed down the
corridor and out the door, I sat at my desk and
vowed a sweet vow: "I would never, never teach
again. I would starve. I would scrub latrines. If
I never, never got my Ph.T. it didn't matter. The
only thing that mattered was that the school year
was over and I had taken a vow. I would never
teach again."

*   *   *   *

The sun shone brightly that whole jobless
summer. "Come September, Anthony encouraged, "I'll
have a teaching fellowship." But "now" was the
discouraging reality.

After weeks of unemployment agencies, followed
by the tracking down of every rumor concerning any
kind of job, we came to the conclusion that it
would be as good a time as any to visit Grandma in
Pennsylvania.

Once in the Keystone State, with Anthony's
sisters taking over the care of the children
somewhat, I found that I had some good, solid
leisure time to devote to a lyrical pursuit of my
Ph.T. — writing poetry.

This time, I was going to be practical about the

whole thing. I bought a book entitled, "How to
Write for Money" by a Jack Woodford and on page
233, I drank in the wisdom of the gods:

"Say you live in Lockjaw, Virginia. You have
written a poem for the first time. What are you to
do with it? Throw the damn thing in the waste-
basket, of course!" So I did. And the trash man
cometh.

But, one day I did write a verse that turned out
to be the only piece of poetry I would ever sell.
A wonderful editor sent me two dollars and fifty
cents for it! It was entitled: "S.O.S." and it
read:

I must hurry to get the dishes washed,
For Junior is at sea.
He's pretendin' he's a-sinkin' fast —
He's workin' furiously . . .
And balin' out my dishwater, —
But now the danger's past.
His lifeboat's safe! All fear's diminished!
My bean-pot stands, — not half-way finished.

Realizing that I had spent more money just
mailing poems than I had made, I took
Mr. Woodford's advice and turned to non-fiction,
concentrating on the how-to type of article, which
Woodford said, had a much better chance of
selling.

One superb attempt was called, "Twenty-five Non-
Messy Ways to Entertain Pre-School Children." With
great pain and detail I elaborated the little
projects that my children and I had embarked on
together to keep us out of each other's hair. We
made Indian villages by turning over conical paper
cups and decorating them. Castles were made from

wrapping small boxes and cans of various shapes and sizes in aluminum foil and grouping them together. A merry-go-round could be made from animal crackers balanced in blobs of peanut butter and arranged on a Lazy Susan, to be eaten later. Using little boxes with pipe-cleaners inserted through them to make bars on cages, with animal cookies placed inside, we fashioned a zoo. On and on I enumerated little ideas until number twenty-five was reached.

When FAMILY CIRCLE sent seventy-five dollars for the article, life was indeed worth living. Cloud Nine kept me aloft for sometime, but my ego descended with a tremendous thud with the publication of the article, "Twelve Ways to Keep Preschoolers Happy!" I had been cut more than 50 percent!

It was about this time that I noticed that every writer's magazine had a theory that the confession-type manuscript was the way for a beginner to earn hard cash. Short stories and articles were supplied by experienced writers, but the confession market was supposedly wide open to the novice and the pay was excellent! The average pay check per "confession" was three hundred dollars. But what to confess?

"You're going to write trash like that?" Anthony objected.

"I'm going to try," I defended.

And so, by day I continued to be ever-lovin', unassuming Mrs. Black, mother of three lovely children, but, by night I became "Claudette Corby," a woman draped in an imaginative black negligee, who sat unceasingly scribbling things like: I WAS A FRIGID WIFE!

The mailman became my problem after we returned to Indiana when he asked, "This here Claudette Corby, who gets her mail here, now — just who is she?"

"A friend, just a friend. She visits us once in a while, usually at night," I replied.

The postman pushed his cap back on his head in a cock-sure gesture with cerebral emanations, "Well now, doesn't she have a home address?"

Undaunted by postmen or editors, however, Claudette kept pouring out her frigid soul, until, one day Anthony fumed, "For heaven's sake, did it ever occur to you that people might think you're writing about us?" It was true. It was time to get rid of Claudette. And so, I put a match to her lovely, lacey, black negligee. I was relieved that the "Frigid Wife" was warm at last when she went up in smoke so painlessly, gracefully and even skillfully.

"And where do you go from here?" my spouse wanted to know, looking up from the Napoleonic Wars, "back to writing poetry?"

"No, I don't think so. I'm going to enter contests again, but this time I'm going to do it the right way by first finding out the secrets of the stars, — the stars being people who have won things like fifty thousand dollars, homes, and trips to Europe."

"And how do you learn their secrets?" the gentleman asked in his tolerating tone.

"By going to the Indiana Contest Convention to be held two weeks from today in Indianapolis!" I announced grandly.

And, out of the depths, Anthony cried to himself, "Oh, Lord, deliver me!"

As we drove into the metropolis of Indianapolis, I asked my contest-friend, Lilian, "Do you suppose we'll really learn anything so far as winning contests are concerned?" (Lil's husband was working on his Ph.D. in sociology at Notre Dame and she was as interested as I in earning her Ph.T.)

We had each left three children apiece back in South Bend under the solicitous care of our respective husbands. No matter how we looked at it we were sure our spouses would profit from their babysitting experience.

As the hotel where the convention was being held loomed into sight, we saw a mammoth red and white banner splashed across the hotel's front which read: "Welcome ODD FELLOWS!"

"That's us," Lil laughed. and we went inside to see if there were many more people like us who couldn't bear to bypass anything that began, "In 25 words or less . . ." There were over two hundred people spending their time and money this particular weekend to learn more about winning contests. Out of the two hundred who attended, the majority were middled-aged women with a sprinkling of about twenty men. As I nostalgically recall, Lil and I were the babies of the convention!

I had fully expected a kind of restful experience, one that would be enlightening contest-wise, but in no way draining on physical stamina. After participating in some 'quickie' soap contest, such as "Name this Picture," (Hellum-Smellum won the prize), the contesters all joined in a kind of Indian War dance, a "honing-up" ceremony for the competition yet to come.

Lil and I were extremely interested in what the contesters had won and how they had gone about winning. One woman had just returned from her prize-winning trip to Bermuda and another fairly new contester had won fifteen hundred dollars, one thousand dollars, and a mink stole all within a period of three weeks. Twelve at the convention had won cars — all in the previous year!

"I won a microwave oven a month ago," said one perturbed contester. "What am I supposed to do with such a thing? I'm scared to death of it!" This was, of course, 1960, when most microwaves were still on drawing boards.

Another woman at the convention said, "I think my entries are clever enough to win prizes, but my secret is to write my entries on a very thick kind of paper and I sometimes turn it sideways, printing very neatly in large letters. I think that my techniques are what calls the judges' attention to them. "Do you ever illustrate your entries?" I asked another big winner.

"Never in a national contest entry," she replied. "But, for a local contest by all means. Dress it up. Sew on it. Cut out pictures, anything that will enhance your point in the jingle or in the 25 words."

"I won ten pairs of roller skates in one month," a woman of sixty-some offered. "And I won a television set, after I had sent in 100 entries!" said another.

"Use alliteration in your entries, but use it subtly!" said a speaker at the convention.

What impressed us most was the quick-thinking cleverness of so many of the conventioneers. The speed with which they could come up with those twenty-five words, — apt, original and sincere, continued to amaze me. I needed peace and quiet — and hours, — before I could come up with anything.

Lil was doing all right for herself. She had won prizes of handkerchiefs, greeting cards, stockings, etc., for last-lines and jingles. A picture of a mother cat carrying a kitten in her mouth and walking across a room she dubbed: 'MEWS' TRAVELS FAST, and won another prize.

And then I won one. The contest was to name a cartoon-drawing of a woman looking askance at a labelless can she was holding in her hand. She had obviously removed the label previously in order to enter a certain contest. Now, she just couldn't recall what was in the can. My name for the cartoon was: THE 'CAN' MUTINY, (a play on the The Caine Mutiny then playing at the movie theaters) and it won last prize — ten unlabeled cans.

On the last day of the convention I won a prize which spurred me on in the following months of prize-privation. It was another naming contest. The picture was of three small boys, all wearing striped coats, in a kind of dance pose, holding out their hats. My title, "MaHatma Dandies" took the first prize — five whole dollars, but to my ego it seemed like five hundred dollars. Imagine! I had topped the conteSTARS! "And everyone of them a 'pro'," I bragged to Anthony later. "You wait and see what I'm going to win in the next few months!"

"I'll wait," he said matter-of-factly. He did. Oh, how he waited until finally prizes began to trickle in.

"Brawny Boy" and "Tawny Joy" — names for two
well-fed looking caricatures who advertised a
chocolate-flavored drink brought me a prize — a
subscription to a comic book!

In trying to win a four year college scholarship
for one of the children — I won an atlas. The
letter began, "This will help you with your
child's education."

And then I went all out trying to "Name the
Matador," a contest that was being sponsored by a
chili con carne maker. "Don Mexicoway" was the
first attempt, then "Cortezesto." The last was
"Bully-Boy." Altogether I sent in ten entries.
Soon an affidavit arrived in the mail to be
notarized. When this was returned, a Nechi
Supernova Sewing Machine was delivered to Black
Manor. "Anthony, I finally won a big prize, isn't
that wonderful?" I exclaimed.

To which His Highness remarked, "Now, if you
could only sew it would be truly wonderful!"

But I couldn't and if I took the time to learn,
there would be no time for entering contests, so
the machine was sold to a dealer.

When a sponsor advertised a contest that would
pay the winner his or her weight in gold I forgot
all about calorie-counters and ate heartily.

Four entries later, I sat back with my banana
split to await the investigator who would soon be
rapping at my door. When a prize is as big as all
that, a man from a detective agency usually stops
to pay a visit, just to make sure you exist, that
you wrote the entry, and that, in case the top
prize is a trip to somewhere, you're not in prison
and unable to pack.

I was indeed a winner. A fourth prize winner! Anthony was excited, "That's pretty close to the top," he said. I hated to admit that there were five thousand fourth place prizes and they were record albums.

A radio was the next award and that was followed by a bicycle from Quaker Oats, all for writing, "When I give oatmeal to my children for breakfast I feel that I have tucked them in for the day!"

"Keep going," Anthony encouraged, "you'll hit the big one yet!" I resharpened my pencils.

Off went twenty-five words on why I like so-and-so baking powder and six weeks later I received an affidavit along with an involved three-paged questionaire and a request to send in, of all things, a picture of myself. Trembling with anticipation, I went to the notary, then to the photographer, and then to the postoffice!

"Why do you suppose they want my picture?" I asked over and over again. Then I would gleefully imagine the newspapers from coast to coast with my picture underneath the caption: BIG WINNER IN THE MIDWEST! TELLS ALL IN TWENTY-FIVE WORDS!

There were only one hundred and four prizes in the baking powder contest — four station wagons and one hundred mixers, complete with juicers.

Weeks went by. Nothing. "Surely," I had said to Anthony for the thousandth time, "they wouldn't have had me go to all that trouble for an old mixer."

"You wouldn't think so," was his assuring reply.

Mentally we took trips back and forth across the country: to Disneyland with the children, then up to New England to see the white birch trees, down to New Orleans for the Mardi Gras — all in our truly marvelous, dream-boat of a station wagon.

And then the letter came! "Congratulations! You have won the super-deluxe mixer . . . ." I could read no more. Tears blocked the vision.

"Your picture must have done it," Anthony commented wryly. When I was about to give him a tart reply he added, "Those judges didn't think anyone as pretty as you could make the most of the sponsor's baking powder in their advertisements. They probably awarded the cars to old-fashioned looking matrons, women who look as though they were born in kitchens. Face it," he continued, "you've already won the biggest prize you'll win in your entire career!"

"I have?" I questioned, blowing my nose.

"Yes," he grinned maliciously, "me!" His shoulder was so comfortable I momentarily agreed.

VI
Stretching the Almighty Dollar

Good news wiped away not only a few stray tears but also any trace of a sniffle as well. Anthony received word that he had passed his candidacy exams for the Ph.D. He was on his way!

For a few wonderful days we were sitting in the catbird seat. In addition, he had found still another job. This one, driving a dump truck for a friend's gravel pit, was a great change of pace. After the haul was over and the gravel had been dumped, the Hoosier Blacks would board the truck for the short trip back to the owner's house. And so, for a time, we literally were riding high. "My Daddy can drive a dump truck!" became Robbie's proud boast.

But jobs from the gravel pit proved to be few and far between, so, we tacked up a notice on one of the University bulletin boards that we were looking for manuscripts to type. My typing speed was good, and Anthony's, even better, but technical theses were too complicated and even Anthony, with his engineering background from the Navy, refused them. Eventually, we got a job typing research work on Thomas More, the English saint, for a professor from Notre Dame who said he

105

would pay us twenty cents a page. But then, the Professor complained about our work saying, "Your typewriter has too large a type and there is also too much space between the lines."

"We can't help it if our typewriter has pica type," I said.

He replied, "Use my typewriter." His elite type could have been dubbed "extra petite" for my money. "Your margins are still too large," he complained. So we adhered to his specified margins, which were the size of an adult earthworm across the beam!

After two months of such semi-microscopic typing, a job for an experienced switchboard operator opened up at the University and Anthony promptly applied.

When Anthony was asked, "Do you know how to run a switchboard?"

He replied coyly, "I've been away from one for a while." (Later he explained to me, "I thought if I could drive a dump truck, I could do almost anything," and his theory proved correct.)

Once again, the first snow fell and the faint jingle of Santa's sleigh-bells could be heard in the distance. Christmas was coming, the geese were getting fat, and so, in order to meet St. Nick head-on, I obtained a job in a big department store for a few weeks.

That first day when I reported to the floor manager, I wondered just what little cog I would be asked to slip into to help with the tremendous Christmas rush.

"A parakeet escaped from our downstairs store," the manager blurted out to me, his moustache quivering with excitement, "go find it!"

I wandered aimlessly, inquiring and looking in every crevice, crack and cranny, with people on all sides calling:

"Miss, would you wait on me? Would you help me with this?"

Having to retort: "I'm sorry, but I can't. I'm looking for a bird!" This brought some unusual responses, but I persisted.

A good hour later, I returned to the manager to report that I could not find the parakeet. "Of course you couldn't," his moustache twitched, "It was found ages ago. Where have you been? Report to the shoe department."

Selling shoes was fun and much easier than I had anticipated. People do bathe and they are not as fussy about squeezing into smaller-sized shoes as cartoons would have you believe. For the first three days, I, saleslady number 103, sold oxfords, sandals, pumps, tennis shoes, Hush Puppies, bowling shoes, baby whites, bedroom slippers, work shoes, and you-name-it shoes. But on the fourth day a growling, teeth-baring man brought me a crumpled, rumpled package and roared:

"Are you Saleslady 103?"

"I was — I am," I quaked, as my half-slip did an about-face.

"Then you're the one I want to see!" he snarled.

"For what reason, sir?" I must keep my cool I told myself.

"Where's the manager? He's gotta see this," he smirked.

"See what?" I managed to squeak. By this time, a miniature crowd had gathered around us.

"See this," he shouted, flinging open the

mangled parcel. Two sensible-looking, brown leather, boys' oxfords dropped from the paper. "Look at-em," the noisy one continued, "Two left shoes!"

The curiosity-seekers looked at the shoes, then at me, then back to the shoes. It was so.

"And she," he pursed his lips again, "sold these to my boy yesterday."

I said I was sorry, very sorry. I didn't know how it happened. "I'll see if I can find the box that must have two right shoes," I said feebly.

"I want my money back," the loud one cut in.

"Besides, that kid of mine wasn't supposed to buy shoes. He was told to wait 'til payday."

The little crowd was beginning to disperse as the manager walked slowly to the cash register to initiate the painful procedure of refunding good, clean money. When the man had gone, the floor manager reminded me that "the customer is always right," at least while he's in the store and chuckled over the whole crazy mess.

I was genuinely relieved when St. Nicholas finally arrived and rescued me.

Then, unexpectedly came another answer to our prayers. A wonderful nun had recommended Anthony and me to a publisher as potential authors of a children's church history series. The Maryknoll Sisters were handling the project and the initial outline was theirs. There were fifty-four subjects, and we had only to write 30,000 words about them!

Since Anthony was the historian in the family, he would do the research. As I had successfully published one children's story, "Tinselette, the

Christmas Angel," and a number of articles on other subjects, I would do the writing. We were on our way!

But lo, we had a deadline to meet and we also discovered to our dismay that we collaborated successfully only in marriage. When it came to writing a church history series and agreeing on which historical facts we should feed to a reading public of fourth, fifth, and sixth graders, we were at constant odds.

When Anthony wrote of early Christian martyrs being covered with tar and tied to high pillars so Nero could set them afire to serve as lamps for his dinner party in the courtyard, I cried "Enough!" I begged, "Let's use another phase of it for the children. This is too gory."

The historian said, "It's history." And the series went on.

Together we cried with Monica, picked clovers with Patrick, chopped down the oak tree with Boniface, and attended the coronation of Charlemagne. We sailed with Leif Ericson, fought at the side of Godfrey of Bouillon, and finally lost our heads completely with Thomas More!

Time had run out! We had failed to meet the deadline of July 10. But the editors were understanding and they magnanimously extended it to July 30, and then to August 10, and finally to the first week in September when the last of it went off to New York.

When it was published, in four attractively illustrated sections, we were truly thrilled! On each cover, in handsome letters, was printed: "ADVENTURES FROM OUR CATHOLIC HERITAGE" by the Maryknoll Sisters.

My inquisitive brother-in-law jokingly asked Anthony, "Which one of the Maryknoll Sisters are you?" But, inside the cover we were given ample professional credit, and the crisp check that accompanied the little series gave us that wonderful feeling one gets from having money in the bank — at least for a little while. But the inevitable rejection slips from editors around the country began appearing once more in manuscripts home-returning. It was Father Philip Hughes, the English historian and well known author, who commiserated with me at a history tea about my recent dearth of acceptances from editors. He, in residence at the time at Notre Dame, of "POPULAR HISTORY OF THE CATHOLIC CHURCH" and "THE REFORMATION" fame, gave this advice:

"My dear," he said in his elegant, British grandfatherly way, with the merriest sparkle in deeply-set, blue eyes, "what you need is a facetious title to accompany anything you've written."

"But nothing I write is accepted lately," I complained, "All I get in the return mail are rejection slips. I've hit a real snag."

"Find a facetious title," he persisted. "I'll give you an example. During World War II, eggs were at a premium in England, and we were consequently rationed one egg per month per person. Now, a good friend of mine who knew a lot about chickens wrote a pamphlet about how to go about increasing a hen's laying power. Only he, who had a real eye for the reading market, titled his pamphlet "How to Make Her Lay" and cleaned up. It sold a million copies. Find a facetious title

for every piece you send out," he repeated.
"Editors will see the joke and go for it, and of
course the people will follow suit!"

The good Father must have brought me luck
because the mailman the next day broke the writing
drought, bringing me prizes from two recent
contest endeavors — a pair of roller skates and a
red leather (empty) billfold. Viewing my paltry
winnings I recalled an Old Irish neighbor's words
to a young woman who had just shown the elderly
lady her new engagement ring.

"It's not the size of it that matters, heaven
knows, even though this one is small enough for
sure," she said in her rich brogue. "But it
represents your young man's efforts, it does, and
that's the importance of it."

The importance of it was simply that defeat or
lack of success in any endeavor was not the worst
of failures. Not to have tried is the true
failure, I kept telling myself.

Keeping up the effort was essential, I
philosophized, and stick-to-it-tiveness was a
virtue I attempted to cultivate along with
frugality.

My paternal grandmother, an immigrant from
Ireland, had the thrifty little habit of filling
paper sacks with sugar whenever she could, hiding
them anywhere in the house, and explaining that
she did this, "'gainst the famine!"

While Grandmother and I had the same end in view
we did use different means to obtain it. With
Anthony doing all the muscle work, I planted a
garden, attempting to raise not sugar cane, but
cucumbers, tomatoes, lettuce, radishes,

muskmelons, corn, and everything-else-that-is-dirt-cheap-at-the-end-of-the-summer-making-you-wonder-why-you-even-bothered.

And, since our three prior attempts to live off the land had netted meager pickings, this time we read the directions on the seed packages and followed them. If they specified one seed to a given hole, we dropped in the one seed, — not three, "to make sure that something comes up," as Anthony reasoned. And we were especially careful with the corn. For three consecutive summers we had planted only a single row because that's all the corn we needed, yet each harvest netted us not one single ear for consumption. After the first year's disaster I suggested we rotate the crop and plant the corn in the area where other vegetables did well. But the second year's crop did no better.

The third summer, the crop came up in snatches squarely down the middle. And it was this third summer's crop that brought no less than nine individuals beating a path to our door to tell us: "That's no way to plant corn. Didn't anyone ever tell you about the birds and the bees — especially the bees?" It was from all these solicitous and observant people we gleaned the essential facts of cross-pollination, — that raising corn is a sexy business.

It was hard trying to understand where all these kindhearted informationists were the years before when each summer our single-rowed corn stood just as high, just as green, and just as barren.

When planting time was over, we sat back to let Mr. Sun and Mrs. Rain get into the act. The tomatoes and cucumbers were great in spite of the corn fiasco, but fortunately for us we were not completely dependent on our crops.

"Do you remember," I asked Anthony, "when we cooked that make-believe turkey for Thanksgiving, when Stephanie was four and Robbie was two and a half?"

"How could I forget?" Anthony answered, amused.

The mock turkey proved to be a most ingenious money-saver. The children kept asking, "Are we going to have turkey? Captain Kangaroo talks about turkeys for Thanksgiving. We are going to have a turkey, aren't we?"

But there was no money in the budget for a turkey. There was only enough money for one cut-up chicken. "Yes, we'll have a turkey," I told them with fingers crossed.

On Thanksgiving morning the stuffing was made as usual, only a bigger glob of it. When it was wet enough it was shaped into a large round ball and placed in the center of the roasting pan.

Then, with the help of a box of toothpicks, the pieces of cut-up chicken were placed at the appropriate positions on the ball of stuffing. True, the little chicken legs, pointing heaven-ward, were dwarfed by the voluminous poultry-seasoned fixin's, but would the children notice? The smell from the oven, accompanied by a sufficiently dark gravy, soon allayed my fears. After a certain amount of basting it was difficult to discern where the chicken left off and the stuffing began. In time was produced a reasonable facsimile, — a Thanksgiving turkey, if you please, in soft candlelight!

Anthony, sharpening the carving knives dramatically, commented on the beautiful table and began the traditional American ritual. He had absolutely no trouble at all carving this type of bird. It simply fell apart as Stephanie squealed in delight.

"Someday," I told Anthony, "I'm going to write an article on how to stretch the mighty dollar. I'm going to include the mock turkey episode and I'm going to write about the necessity of having an understanding grocer."

"And how do you define an 'understanding' grocer?" Anthony asked.

"He is a kind man, like our grocer, who will hold a check until payday when it means what it says," I answered. "He is also the helpful type who will steer you to the best bargains in his store and away from pseudo-bargains. He will also let you know which bread is the freshest, which meat the stretchingest, which watermelons the sweetest . . . ."

"You could also include in your article," Anthony added, "how to make canteens for day-campers out of ketchup bottles." Anthony was speaking of a recent endeavor in which Stephanie and her little friend, Pam, had wanted to go to day camp together. The people who ran the camp issued a set of instructions stating everything a child would need, — canteen, knife, etc. Included in the instructions, for those who wished to improvise, were directions for making a canteen using an old towel and an empty ketchup bottle. So, I followed the directions and made one for Stephanie.

Pam, on the other hand, had been taken to town
and fully equipped with the best of everything.
Her new knife shone in its all-leather holster
while Stephanie's paring knife hung at her side in
a makeshift belt.

Pam was intrigued with Stephanie's home-
fashioned gadgets. "Gosh, Stephanie," she
confided, "you're lucky to have a canteen like
that. A ketchup bottle is neat. I wish I had a
ketchup-bottle-canteen like that."

"Yes," Stephanie agreed with her friend. "It's a
neat idea and it works real well. The water even
tastes like ketchup!"

But, getting back to the subject of stretching
the almighty dollar, — knowing how to plant corn,
making mock turkey, devising hundreds of ways to
cook hamburger, spaghetti, etc., and finding a
patronizing grocer ... all are ways to beat the
budget before it beats you. Added to these is the
basic thing of all, -- improvisation.
Improvisation is the realization that if you
haven't something that you need, you make as if
you do!

My classic example of improvising happened years
ago one weekend when Anthony's mother and father
announced they would visit us accompanied by
Anthony's two sisters. They would come Friday
night, take in the Notre Dame game Saturday
afternoon and return to Pennsylvania the next day.
They would stay with us, of course, in Vetville.
Then, suddenly, two cousins decided to do the same
thing and word was received that still more
relatives were to visit us for the game. They said
they would stay at motels, but what few people

*Sidewalks form an interesting pattern where
the Fieldhouse once stood.*
Photo by Brother Martinus Bombardier, C.S.C.

seem to understand (who do not live in the vicinity of the South Bend-Mishawaka area) is that motel and hotel reservations on football Saturdays must be made months in advance. The likelihood of anyone succeeding in obtaining space in any motel accommodation was and is nil. Vetville accommodations would have to be stretched and stretched and stretched. We borrowed beds. The big problem was, however, not having enough sheets to cover so many beds.

"Go buy some," Anthony advised. "Our charge is good at Sear's."

But why, I reasoned, invest for a single day or night when it might not be necessary. "I'm not going to run up a bill," I told Anthony, "I'll think of something."

I counted what I had and counted again. Yes, I could do it. I would do it. There was a way. And the budget would remain intact. The relatives came, and within a few hours discovered what we were all aware of, — there was no room for them at any motel. They would have to bed down with the Black's in Vetville, on borrowed cots and foam-rubber on the floor.

Later, when the late news was over and the late-late movie digested, unit 35-A became reasonably quiet. The chirrup-chirrups of a displaced cricket, the confident hums of the refrigerator, the wooden joints cracking occasionally — gave evidence that night-time was upon us and star-dust was dispersing itself silently but surely.

In the bedrooms, blankets were spread and pillows fluffed. And when the light finally went out, I chuckled to myself: "I'm home free." In my mind I blessed the fact that I was married to an absent-minded professor who didn't know a white bedsheet from an Irish linen tablecloth! He hadn't even noticed! And neither had anyone else.

But then my bed-partner interrupted my reverie. Rolling over to my side of the foam rubber in an apparent attempt to deliver a confidential message, he said, "Excuse me, but when you get time, please pass the mustard!"

The jig was up! The light went on! My curlers stood on end!

"How did you know?" I wanted to know.

"Does a leopard have spots?" the professor demanded, pointing to the tablecloth. There, under the direct glow of the lamp, were the hardly-discernible designs of shiny-threaded bunches of grapes, woven artistically into the beautiful cloth! My improvisation was as bare as a skinned banana!

But the adults in the house were not the only ones exhibiting originality. Stephanie and Robbie were at the moment going through the neighborhood selling "beauty" rocks gleaned from the cemetery behind the house. Cemetery rocks went for anywhere from one cent to three cents, depending on the inherent beauty of each. Earlier they had sold cherries by the dozen from the only tree in the backyard. A customer could buy the cherries, arranged precisely in discarded egg cartons, one cherry to each mold, for two cents a dozen. Bonanza!

Anthony was now a teaching fellow at Notre Dame and was tasting first hand the joy of sharing the Napoleonic Wars with college age students. His hours were few however, and, consequently, so were the dollars.

I was busy putting my thoughts on paper about "Stretching the Almighty Dollar" when the phone rang.

"Mrs. Black," said the secretary from the University of Notre Dame, "I'm calling several homes within walking distance of the University, to ask if those who have rooms for rent would take in nun-students who are working on their graduate degrees and who must establish residence here, rather than regular male students as in the past. You know that since this is a man's University, there are no facilities for them to live on campus. We have to refuse many nun-students each year because so few families will open their homes to them. When you consider that they don't smoke, or drink, and you do know how desperately we need good, well-trained sisters in our schools . . . ."

Here indeed was a well-worded, worthy plea! "Well . . .," I stammered.

"Well, I do have a baby . . . ."

"The nuns would love it!" said the convincing-one. "Think of their maternal instincts!"

I did, and thought how it would be nice to give mine a rest for a change. "Well," I concluded . . ., "I have no objections, really, but I will have to talk it over with my husband before I give a final go-ahead. This is his house, too, you know."

"Take a week or two to think and talk it over," she concluded, "then call me." And the voice was gone.

It was certainly something to think about. As a

young girl I had seriously considered entering the convent. Now the convent was coming to me!

Then came Anthony's reaction, "What will my life be like around here with all those women?" Anthony was aghast. "They'd probably get up at five and go to bed at ten and we'd have to tiptoe around. Look, my aunt is a nun and I have had nuns as teachers. But to live in the same house with them?" Anthony stewed. "It will take more than a week to think this one over."

"I hope they do stay here," Stephanie confided, "they can help me with my homework."

By the end of the week we were all convinced that living with nuns would be a unique experience, and one that we would all profit from in one way or another. "Just think of their good influence," I reminded my family.

"I'm thinking . . .," Anthony commented.

"We will have room for three nun-students!" I told the Notre Dame secretary.

"God bless you!" she replied.

During the next few days I began to be especially friendly to a woman who lived at the end of our block, a landlady who had had under her roof no less than four nuns at a time for the past several years. "Do you find them hard to live with?" I asked.

"At first, yes," she replied. "But I've gotten so that I enjoy their company. It used to be that I would find myself having my nightly bottle of beer about midnight and then hiding the empty underneath my bed, but now I have it at seven or eight in the evening. In fact, one nun joins me occasionally. One of the Sisters I had, though, was a Superior of some kind in her community, and it took a little doing until she finally realized that this was my house and I ran it as I pleased. She was the kind whose advice was more like commands. Then, there was one who used to make flying novenas . . . ."

"Flying novenas?" I repeated, thinking I was getting into more than I had asked for.

"Yes . . . You know, she'd set her alarm to go off every hour on the hour and say a special prayer, — for nine straight hours . . . ."

"I never heard of them, — nine day novenas maybe, but . . . ."

"Well these are the flying kind, — in nine hours you're all done but then, so is the rest of the house!"

Pushing the baby stroller back home I was not as confident that having nuns as roomers was going to be as simple as I had originally thought. But why worry? Hadn't I know slews of Sisters from every kind of Order? I had usually gotten along with them just fine . . . but then again, I hadn't lived with them.

A few weeks later the 'God-bless-you' secretary from Notre Dame was on the phone. "Mrs. Black, I have news!" she began. "The University is renovating an old building on campus as a dormitory for the nuns, and it will be finished by the time school starts."

"So I won't have Sisters for roomers?" I asked.

"That's right," she answered. "The dormitory will hold about forty-five and, so far, we have only twenty-three applications for year-round residence for those in graduate school . . . but,

Mrs. Black, since you were so kind, we will see that your rooms are filled with boys when the semester begins. In fact, you're the first on our list. As soon as a student asks about a room, I'll send him down . . . ."

In a matter of minutes we had switched not only the sex, but also the lifework and vocations of my roomers. So, I put away the feminine-looking dresser scarves and got out the plain ones and awaited the male students the gods were sending us.

"I don't know if I'm glad or sad," I said to Anthony. "I do believe it would have been interesting to have had three nun graduate-students. Now, we'll never know."

VII
The Belles of St. Mary's

"How much longer will it take the British Army to get to 1914?" I asked Anthony one evening, when he was literally knee-deep in research. (The subject of Anthony's doctoral dissertation was "The British Army, 1902-1914.")

Books, hundreds of notes, and stacks of papers formed a colosseum around him. "They've been to 1914 and back to 1902 again," he said, smiling.

"Does this mean that the dissertation won't be too long getting done now?" I questioned.

"Not exactly. It will still take some doing, but I was over at the University Placement Center this afternoon and found out some interesting information," he continued.

"Like?" I prompted.

"Well, I learned that many universities and colleges will hire a teacher if he or she has everything done — all the credits, the language requirements, the candidacy exams — everything completed but the thesis. I've got all these things, plus two bachelors' degrees, a Master's degree, and a candidacy for the Ph.D. What I'm saying is that I'm going to apply for a teaching position and work on the dissertation on the side.

123

124

It's possible and it's being done all over the country."

It was a grand speech, one I had been waiting years to hear. "So, what's keeping you?" I cried. "Where are the application blanks?"

"Some have already been filled out," Anthony replied, smugly. "And, I had my picture taken — 24 pictures for three dollars to send around." There was jubilation in his voice as he asked, "Will you help me type more letters of application?"

The job was the important thing. We would go wherever required to produce the all-necessary bread and butter. And so the letters were written and placed in the mail. "If the University of Pittsburgh needs an historian," I commented one afternoon, licking the glue on an envelope, "we would be near friends and relatives, and that would be nice."

Soon, twenty-four letters were ready to accompany the twenty-four photos. Twenty-four letters of hope. One week later we had our first answer. "Open it!" I cried. The waiting was difficult. The contents were disappointing. A little college in Ohio appreciated hearing from us. But, there was no opening.

One by one the replies trickled in: "Sorry — no opening." One disgruntled head-of-a-history department wrote, "Sorry, you're in the wrong field. If you had studied science, now, you'd have it made. Every year college presidents find more and more reasons to eliminate more and more history from the college curriculum. I'm lucky to have my job — I'm the last one left here . . . ."

It was true. There was such an emphasis on science, ever since Sputnik went up, that history wasn't being taught as such in elementary schools anymore. The arts were in eclipse. Was there anyone out there yet who just might be interested in the British Army, 1902-1914? It didn't seem likely. And the weeks went by.

"If you don't find something," I said, "maybe I could go back to teaching myself . . . ."

"No ma'm," he was adamant, "something will turn up. If I have to, I can teach second grade."

"You wouldn't be hired," I told him truthfully, "because you haven't the proper education credits."

"I can teach college, but not second grade. That's ridiculous!"

When things looked their blackest black, a phone call from across the Dixie Highway cleared the air! "Could you come over for an interview?" said the voice on the other end of the line. Could he!

"That was St. Mary's College," he told me. "The head of the history department said that they may need someone and she'd like to talk to me."

I got out his whitest shirt. "Don't look too anxious, now," I cautioned, "play a little hard to get."

"Good heavens woman! I'm desperately in need of a job and you say play hard to get!"

"I'm just trying to calm you down," I replied.

"What would you teach over there, Daddy?" Robbie asked, standing in the bedroom doorway, attired in full pirate regalia.

"I'd teach history," Anthony answered.

"You'd teach girls," Robbie corrected. "Don't just girls go to St. Mary's?"

"Girls have to know about history, too," Anthony explained. "That's why your Mother fights such a good battle — she knows her history," he concluded. And he was off . . . .

Seconds before he was to meet the head of the history department, the president of the college, the renowned poet, Sister Madeleva, C.S.C., and the Mother Superior of the Order, Anthony made a disillusioning discovery! A huge wad of bubble gum, that he had evidently sat on in the car (a little homey reminder) was adhering tenaciously to the back of his pants!

Tugging desperately, he managed to free one stringy portion and shoved it into the nearest coat pocket, but the remainder had to stay. He had no other choice but to pull up his pants, pull down his coat, and hope the sisters liked the odor of Double Bubble!

Two hours later a confident, smiling Anthony returned. "I got the job! I got the job!" he was exuberant. "Meet Instructor Black," he hammed to the children. Then, remembering, he frowned and said: "Who left the bubble gum in the car?"

"Are you really going to teach at St. Mary's?" Stephanie wanted to know.

"Girls!" Robbie was incredulous.

"How many girls go there?" I inquired.

"Roughly, around one thousand I believe," he smiled. "And it's growing yearly."

"There's only one thing about this job I'm not going to like," he continued.

"What's that?" I wanted to know.

"What do I do when a lovely young thing comes crying to me about a low grade I've given her?"

"That's your problem," I smiled, thinking of
what was in store for my soft-hearted husband. But
then came the best thought of all! "Why, we won't
even have to move! We can stay right here in this
nice big house!"

"And I'm still close enough to my resources for
the dissertation. The University of Chicago is
ninety minutes away — and I can take a trip to
D.C. and the Library of Congress. It's not like
I'll be in California," the new Instructor was
excited.

But suddenly he frowned. "You know," he
confessed, "I don't know much about the St. Mary's
girls. I see them at the football games, waving
their white handkerchiefs . . . ."

"But you will learn, my dear," I said,
consolingly. "We'll all learn."

And away in the distance I heard the bells of
St. Mary's ringing in the first wave of evening.

*   *   *   *

When September and the school year dawned
Anthony crossed the highway to the beautiful world
of St. Mary's College. The graciousness of the
nuns, the high academic standing of the
institution, and the majestic buildings, all made
a tremendous impact on the fledgling professor.

As the first weeks went by his initial timidity
at teaching in a women's college lessened. Soon,
he was chiding me at breakfast with: "Now, hurry
with the toast. My girls are waiting!"

When November came, Anthony was dismayed as he
told me "You know, the St. Mary's students wear a

Church of Loretto.

Holy Cross Hall.

Haggar College Center, Lake Marion.
Photo by Gary E. Mills

LeMans Hall.

A favorite place to relax and study.

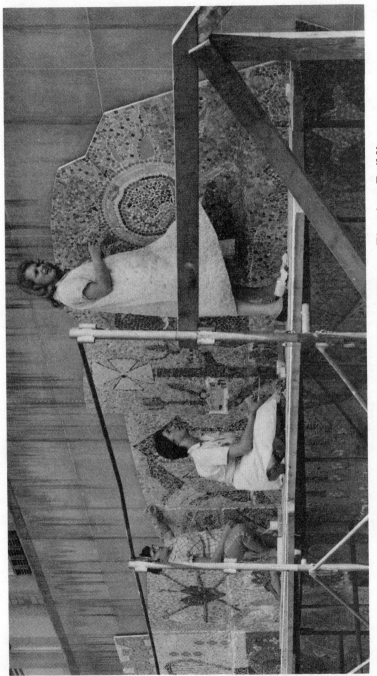

St. Mary students working on mosaic on Moreau Fine Arts Building.

kind of light-colored uniform — pastel shades. I
suppose they're allowed to pick their favorite
color, provided it's a pastel shade of blue,
yellow, green, or pink."

"Well, I got used to all this colorama, or
whatever, but today, what a shock. I walked into
my classroom and there everyone was wearing a grey
suit! No more colors. Just solid grey! They said
it was their winter garb. It really threw me for a
minute. I thought I was in the wrong school."

As for me, the school year meant I was once
again a full-time landlady. This year I had two
chemical engineering graduate students sharing our
home with us and in addition to the title
"Landlady" was added a new title, "Chaperon."

Mr. and Mrs. Black were to chaperon the Senior
Nocturne, the Junior Bunny Hop, and the Sophomore
Social, — all new duties for us from St. Mary's
College.

The first invitation lay undiscovered in
Anthony's coat pocket for two weeks. I discovered
it in just enough time to borrow a white and blue
gown from a neighbor, dye a pair of white gloves
blue and tweeze my renegade eyebrows.

But lack-a-day! Cinderella had stayed by her
chimney too long! Upon entering the Le Man's
dining room, now decorated as an elegant ballroom,
it was discovered that all the Belles of St.
Mary's were resplendently regal in short-length,
ballerina type evening gowns.

"If only I could cut a yard or two off from this
floor-length antique, or go home and read a
fashion magazine," I mumbled to Anthony.

To which Anthony replied, "How did we turn into

old fuddy-duddies in so few years." One glance at Anthony, and it was confirmed. His outfit was even worse than mine. He was clad in a large-lapeled, padded-shouldered, navy blue tuxedo, which we had purchased for fifteen dollars at the "Operatunity" Shoppe in Pittsburgh (a second-hand clothing store run by Pittsburgh Opera Company devotees), years before.

"You'd think a "Senior Nocturne" would be nocturnal," I said as flashing lights conspired to show us off as the one couple in the history department who believed in re-living history.

When the Junior Hop came along, however, we were better prepared. I had since become acquainted with a neighbor who subscribed to VOGUE.

"Tres chic, Madame," Anthony smiled. I had taken his arm but dropped it in amazement when the Chairman of the Dance greeted us at the door of the Stapleton Lounge which had been decorated as a Louis XIV ballroom!

The chairman was a beautiful girl, who in addition to the popular shorty evening gown, had on only one earring! To be sure, it was a large earring, but still it was just one earring. Her hair, on the side with the earring, was combed back, away from the face. But, on the earring-less side, the hair half covered the ear. Had I goofed again?

But no, not completely. For there, just a few feet away, was a history student wearing two earrings, big as life.

"Your evening is a success," Anthony was saying, but he spoke too soon. Even before the "Good-night, Ladies" dance was announced, a sweet young thing came over to us and requested that we give a talk in four weeks at the Senior Marriage Institute.

"On what subject, specifically?" Anthony asked.

"On the budget, on how you two manage money in marriage," was the reply.

"We've never had any to speak of to manage," he confided.

"Well," the student continued, "we've got a priest telling us about the Sacrament of Matrimony, a doctor talking on the physical aspect of it all, and a psychologist to handle the mental business . . . ."

"And you're giving us the budget," Anthony concluded. "That's like asking Martin Luther to give a lecture on the Papacy!"

"We'll be glad to do it. Sounds like fun," I reassured her. Our speeches were consequently prepared, with Anthony building his talk around actual figures, like how much money it takes to keep a family of five in milk per month, and what the average obstetrician charges to deliver a baby, while my talk was built around personal experiences, like how I am capable of whipping up a batch of oatmeal chowder the day before payday, and how I keep getting new babies when what I really should be getting is a new coat.

On the night of the lectures, my talk got off to a particularly bad start. Attempting to classify things, I unwittingly stated: "I was not a St. Mary's girl. I was a Seton Hill woman!" When the hooting, lady-like-enough to-be-sure, but hooting, nevertheless, subsided, I went on with my talk.

"That part about the coat must have got to them," Anthony said later. "They gave us a check."

I was elated. To be paid twenty-five dollars for talking. Imagine!

And life at St. Mary's and at Black Manor went on, with Anthony occasionally and absent-mindedly wearing a brown coat with blue pants or vice-versa, and constantly having color consultations with me on which tie to wear with what and why.

The girls were proving to be excellent students. "No discipline problems," Anthony would boast, "except possibly the click-click of knitting needles at times."

Joining whole-heartedly into the faculty wives' organization along with the women faculty members was a bit difficult with small children. There were too many bridge games and enterprises held in the afternoons when available baby-sitters were busy with high school. But once in a while something came up in an evening that warranted the effort of getting out of the house. "An evening with the St. Mary's Foreign Students" seemed like something I should participate in. And I did.

Hostess faculty members asked volunteers like myself to single out one foreign student to spend a large part of the evening with to explain American customs, etc., and to sit with the student at the table.

"I'll take that young Japanese girl over there," I said.

"Go to it," said the hostess.

After introducing myself and finding out the student's name I dove headlong into the business at hand. We discussed the United Nations, St. Mary's, the weather, and, finally, I thought it was time to get on with American customs.

138

"It's turkey on Thanksgiving," I began, and came up for air when I got to the why's of hanging Christmas stockings. After I attempted to explain Auld Lang Syne, paper hats and noisemakers I said, "Now it's your turn, tell me about Japanese customs."

"I know very few," she confided. "You see I was born and grew up in Mishawaka, Indiana, just a few miles from here."

*   *   *   *

And life went on. Anthony enjoyed teaching, but while other families took up oil painting or ceramics or gardening, the only thing we took up was the mortgage. Like almost every teaching position at every college in the country in the fifties, Anthony's job at St. Mary's paid about half of what other professions paid.

"They'll double teachers' salaries in ten years," Anthony kept repeating, "you'll see. And, remember I'll get a big raise as soon as my Ph.D. dissertation gets in."

But the statistics were most discouraging. A Notre Dame graduate in Business Administration (an undergraduate degree) had just been hired by the Caterpillar Company at a salary of five thousand dollars. Anthony's starting salary at St. Mary's, with a B.A., B.S., M.A. and Doctoral Candidate status, was three thousand two hundred dollars and this amount was in line with salaries across the country. Sayings such as "living in genteel poverty" and "threadbare professors" began to be understood.

But then, I always had my contesting to fall back on. What secretly worried me, however, was the fact that a recent dog-food company contest had awarded ten thousand miniature palm trees as last prizes, and even though I sent in a fair number of entries, I had not even won a leaf!

Desperately searching for something of a more lucrative and predictable nature than winning contests, I took to reading want ads. At summer's end I found one worthy of being read aloud to my beloved spouse:

"Experienced kindergarten teacher needed at once for church kindergarten. Half day sessions."

"So?" Anthony asked.

"So, nothing," I answered. "It's an interesting want ad for a kindergarten teacher."

"But you're not a kindergarten teacher," he continued his reasoning, "so why do you find it so interesting?"

"Well, maybe it wouldn't hurt to apply out of curiosity," the wheels were grinding.

"You'd never be hired," he said sullenly, and then added, "and have you forgotten you vowed you'd never teach again?"

"But this is for only half day sessions, and this is kindergarten, not second grade . . . ."

"And this is worse," Anthony interrupted, "if they crawled on the floor in second grade, they'll probably crawl on the ceiling in kindergarten! Besides," he added, "don't talk so silly. What would Mary Kay do without you?"

Of course he was right. But the ad was interesting. And without that dissertation being completed, Anthony's salary was so very small.

The next evening the ad was there again. Big as
a billboard, with the NEEDED AT ONCE almost
spurring me to action. "I could call, just to see
what the salary is," I reasoned. But my conscience
interfered. "You're no kindergarten teacher; you
have a secondary license and you're not
experienced with this age group save for your own
children. And what about Mary Kay? Stephanie and
Robbie would be in school. But Mary Kay needs a
mother at home with her. But then," I fluctuated
back again, "the ad will be gone tomorrow."

But the next evening, there it was again! And, I
had just thought of a wonderful friend who just
loved Mary Kay and could also use the extra money
for babysitting with her.

Yes, I would call — just to let them know that
a teacher, not a kindergarten teacher, but a
teacher, nevertheless, had seen and read their
well-worded plea . . . .

"You say you've taught second grade?" the voice
at the other end repeated. "Would you come out for
an interview?"

"Come out? Yes!" I exclaimed.

Later that day, I learned that "out" was really
out, for I went out to the cows, the clover, the
pigs, the mud, out to the tractors, the corn, the
red and white barns, the unpaved roads, out to the
country with its friendly people.

"I'm not a Methodist, I'm a Catholic," I
commented to the kindergarten board members.

"That's perfectly all right," a twentieth
century voice of religious toleration answered,
"This is run like a kindergarten in a public
school. There are children of all faiths who

attend. We simply use the church basement for our classes."

Before you could say "John Wesley" there I was sharpening pencils, cutting paper and sorting out pipe cleaners, readying myself and my props for kindergarten down in the basement of a Methodist Church which was well over one hundred years old.

Then the children came, twenty-one of them, all in varying degrees of helplessness. And with the children the all-essential paraphenalia of too large or too small boots and rubbers, of snug and not-so-snug snow-pants, of zippers that were occasionally on track but mostly off-track, and stuck.

By consulting several kindergarten teacher-friends and by guidance received at the local library, I organized my mornings into Show and Tell Time, or, Sharing Time as it is sometimes called, Story Hour with both books and records, a heavenly time called Recess, a Library Period for books to take home, and a time devoted to music and art.

Art was a challenge I met head-on. With paste, scissors, construction paper, clay and hundreds of Ding Dong School T.V. lessons behind me, I couldn't miss.

With music, I began by resurrecting all my old piano scales and recital pieces and gradually my renditions of the nursery rhymes became recognizable. There was even one piano selection I knew from memory that was just the thing needed to emphasize correct drum rhythm. The difficulty with it was that I could recall only the very beginning of the piece. Each day I would ask the drummer to beat along with me as I began to plow through the boom-ta-ta, boom-ta-ta. And when I reached the point where my memory faded I would simply turn around and say, "Fine! Now let's try it over again!" And we'd begin all over and play the music together until we reached the same spot again.

Years hence I pictured one after the other of my kindergarten pupils being led to a psychoanalyst's couch and complaining: "But Doc, I think everything would have been okay, — if only that kindergarten teacher would have finished playing that one piece!"

I found, however, that I had a tremendous advantage over other first-fling kindergarten teachers in that Robbie was attending a morning kindergarten class in a public school in the city. We usually would arrive home at approximately the same time and invariably my first question would be the same one that mothers all over the country ask when their offspring comes through the door.

"What did you do today in school?" Only my question was asked with an additional purpose in mind.

If Robbie had a pudding party one week, we'd be sure to have one the next. Things he seemed to be enthusiastic about I was careful to include in my own program.

Perhaps the most interesting time of all was Sharing Time, when the little boys and girls brought in everything but the kitchen sink to Show and Tell about. Some days were jackpot days, days when there were twelve puppy-dogs to see and feel, days when there were "real" movies shown of a family vacation, while other less spectacular times were spent in listening to a shy girl tell about how she lost her tooth, or to a constant talker-showoff who wanted to display his new shoes, or tie, or pants, for the hundredth time.

It was during Sharing Time that a near-calamity threatened the calm of my kindergarten. I was busily trying to help a little girl replace her blocks in her half-torn box when I suddenly became aware of what the current Sharing Time performer was "sharing."

"And here," the child was saying majestically, his pants on their way down, "is the scar from my hernia operation!"

I got there in time. With one hand holding the most vital section of pants, I pointed out a tiny section of the scar with the other, talked very rapidly about what a wonderful patient the child had been in the hospital, how fast he had recovered, how glad we were that he was back with us again, and then, finally, I managed to close the zipper with a whispered, "Amen!"

Show and Tell time produced interesting notes to the homes such as:

Dear Mother,

I trust by now you have missed your girdle and bra. Sandra had a most enthusiastic audience today for Show and Tell, I assure you.

Sincerely,
Mrs. Black

and,

Dear Mother,

I understand that someone in your relationship is going to fashion a bracelet

for you from your gallstones.
Congratulations! There may be an empty spot
now on our science table, but — our loss is
your gain! Perhaps Johnny could bring in the
jewelry at a later date for Show and Tell
time. This is at your discretion.

Sincerely,
Mrs. Black

and, on a different subject,

Dear Mother,

I wouldn't worry about the results of
the interest test. The fact that Robert came
out under "Shepherd" is no reason to believe
that he will not be gainfully employed in
his future as an adult.

Sincerely,
Mrs. Black

The days and weeks sailed by as my kindergarten
work proved enjoyable. The Ph.D. and Ph.T. were
truly coming along. The board members who
sponsored the kindergarten proved to be especially
congenial people, particularly the treasurer who
requested that the kindergarteners pay their
tuition by putting the checks in the empty milk
bottles outside their respective kitchen doors, —
he being also the principal milkman of the little
community.

Soon, spring was here and we began, the
kindergarteners and I, working hard on what would
eventually be our main performance for the year.
Ours would be a patriotic program from early
American times, a little play, featuring the
Minuet dance. But now I had a problem, one which I
had not anticipated when I began the fall

"Children, the Minuet is this way — hold your hands up, together, now it's IN, and now it's OUT . . .," but the difficulty at the moment was the fact that I had trouble exemplifying the IN because I just couldn't get close enough.

The board insisted I finish the year providing I felt up to it. The baby was not due until late summer and so I did. But the questions came.

"Is it true you're going to have a baby?"

"My mother told me that you were on the nest, but I don't see any!"

"Here, I bought these booties for the baby."

With the final curtsy of the Minuet on program-night I knew that the end of my career as a kindergarten teacher was at hand. I had enjoyed the children and it had helped tremendously toward my Ph.T. There was now the summer ahead and I had only to have my baby, be once again a full-time mother, and spend my free time wondering how else I could supplant the kindergarten income.

If you have ever been approximately nine months pregnant you know that it is pure folly to think that you are capable of filling many job openings. The only opening you can unquestionably fill is the hole in the maternity skirts, just below the 'eternity' jacket. So, since I had impressed myself with this fact, I decided that the actual supplanting of my kindergarten salary was impossible. I could not at the present time 'make' money. I could only save it. Or at least, try to.

Meanwhile, back in the hospital, I had my new baby. This time it was a boy and we called him Bernard Morrow after my father. Since my Dad had spent a good part of his life playing and coaching football, it was fitting that his namesake be a full-back at the start, weighing in at nine pounds seven ounces. Our cross-pollination had again netted a blonde.

Someone once said that the more children you have the nicer they become. Perhaps this is because all mistakes are made on the first few, parents learning by doing, so to speak. Whatever the sayings, with Bernard Morrow, we as parents hit the jack-pot!

Here was a temperament honed by virtue. Here was a gentleness, a kindness, an integrity, a patience, a trust, a unique love exhibited and given freely to his older brother and sisters so special that years later, behind his back, these siblings would refer to Bernard as "saint."

"No matter what I do to him," reported Mary Kay, two years older, "when he gets in my way and I don't want him to play with me, he just takes it!"

"I never heard him say anything bad about anyone," Stephanie contributed.

"He's a great little brother," Robbie smiled affectionately.

However marvelous Bernard's prognosis for the future was, the grandfather whose name he bore was to share in his babyhood only six short months. But they were happy months and we were exceedingly grateful we had them.

VIII
A Strike and a Spare and Then Some

Life and living suddenly became full of decisions, sorrow, and turmoil with the comparatively sudden death of my father.

When we buried him, on a high knob of a little upgrade in a cemetery overlooking the Pennsylvania countryside, it was a kind of triumphal march on a glowing, sun-filled morning. He had gone to his rest and reward, and we laid him beside his father, an immigrant from Belfast, and an infant son who bore his name.

In the months following his death, there were understandably, changes to be made. There was his business, an eight lane bowling business to be specific.

"I don't want to run it myself," Mother said after many weeks of careful consideration. "Yet, I'd hate to see it leave the family. It's a good established bowling alley . . . ."

Anthony and I, being four hundred miles away, didn't seem to be able to do anything about it. Besides, when we considered the trauma and effort invested in Anthony's education, operating a bowling alley had a futile element to it.

My sisters and their husbands considered and

reconsidered the possiblity of taking over the business, but they reached the same conclusion, — it just was not feasible for them to make a change. So, as Mother sadly negotiated the sale of the business, a brainstorm hit Anthony and me at the same time.

Hadn't a reliable friend of the family's offered to manage the business for Mother if she chose to run it? Would he consider managing it for us instead? This would give Anthony the time needed to complete his contract with St. Mary's and possibly to complete his Ph.D. before we elected to move to Pennsylvania.

Thus, the deal was made that we would buy the business and pay mother a given sum each month out of the bowling receipts until the purchase price was paid in full. This was a tremendous thing! Now, we had in our very hands a "money making machine." Could we now forget about tutoring athletes, renting rooms, doing substitute teaching, etc., to keep our heads above water?

There was little time to speculate and much work to do. There was the manager's schedule and salary to be figured out, pin-boys and pin-girls to recruit (this was before automatic pinsetters were popular), and rest rooms to renovate.

Mother helped with suggestions, gave us old receipts to study and offered many words of encouragement. The pop man, candy man, pin refinishing man, towel man, — all became our new acquaintances along with the captains of the various bowling leagues.

"Why is it that last year eight lanes weren't enough for your league, and this year you want only six? Is there something wrong?" Anthony asked one of the league-captains.

"Not exactly," she answered with a smile. "It's just that one-third of our bowling league is pregnant right now. In January we'll be up to eight lanes again!"

New red step pads were tacked into place. Light fixtures were washed and replaced. Bowling balls were polished and the alleys themselves sanded and refinished. Our first bowling season was upon us!

With fingers crossed, we put a little extra wax on the new counter, said a fervent prayer that the final coat of enamel in the Ladies' Room would be dry in time for the first customer, and trepidatiously opened the front doors.

The beginning weeks were poor ones. "We're not doing as well as your father did this same time last year," Anthony commented after viewing Daddy's records.

Mother clarified the situation by saying, "But the weather was cool then, just right for bowling, and we didn't have a steel strike to contend with." The phone rang sometimes to reserve alleys, and sometimes it did not. While the balls rolled over the highly polished wood, and the strikes and spares were marked in black, waxy squares and triangles on the score sheets, the cash register jingled and, once in a while, it jangled. Soon, the calendar said that it was time for Anthony to get back to South Bend and "his girls." So we gave the keys to the manager, said adieu to our families, and headed back to South Bend.

Gradually, as the steel strike ended and the bowling season gained momentum, the bank deposits mounted. "Can you imagine," said Anthony in amazement, "even after all the bills are paid, we still have money in the bank?"

In the meantime, while Anthony taught his classes by day and whipped the British Army into shape by night, the washing machine heaved, sighed, and was no more.

"It's not worth fixing," said a repairman. "It's too old."

So, we made arran-ements to buy a new one. After filling out an ap⸍⸍⸍ication for financing we awaited its delivery, but the phone rang and the man at the bank told Anthony that they could not help us with it because of a loan we already had with them. "On your salary," the man said, "we feel, you've got all you can handle."

"I see," was all Anthony said. "Well, if that's the case, then I'll just have to pay cash for it!"

"We couldn't afford to eat bread," I thought to myself, "so we'll eat cake." And what glorious cake!

A trip to town and new outfits for the children! New boots! And some life insurance of my very own! "To think that I can now afford to die," I remarked to Anthony.

"You look healthy as a horse," he replied. "You're throwing money down the drain."

Once a month, Anthony took the late train to Pennsylvania to the bowling alley to relieve his manager for a spell, throw a few balls down the lanes, and of course, to count the money.

Slowly, but surely, we turned in the direction of solvency. What we could not know at this point was that neighborhood bowling businesses, like neighborhood movie houses, would eventually become labeled as belonging to a by-gone era.

The onslaught of television had a profound effect on the recreational businesses in general, but until pro football and basketball games began to dominate weekends, there was still enough of the pie to go around for the remaining competition.

As people discovered they could watch first rate movies or a highly talented professional ball team at home, for free, old fashioned bowling alleys, as ours, began to disintegrate at a rapid rate. To compete, one now needed a multi-million dollar facility at the "right location."

In the interim, however, there was yet time to make some cold hard cash. So at least for several years, the business pie's flavor was rich, smooth and delicious. And we were grateful to my parents for the opportunity of savoring it.

*   *   *   *

Since returning to South Bend, however, a "now or never" attitude regarding the dissertation permeated the air. And the tediousness of it all, the strung-out drudgery was getting to me.

"I don't know why you're doing so much moaning about this thesis, Virginia," said Anthony. "Sure, it's taking a long time to complete. But, I'm still lucky at that. I found a subject that can at least be researched in this country. I could have had to go to England for primary resources."

"All this writing and rewriting is a stupid chore," I complained. "Five hundred pages of what?

The British Army! Who cares about the British
Army? Who cares if it marches down into the sea
tomorrow? Why, all of it is downright un-
American!"

"You're just frustrated," said Anthony, whose
rank was now assistant professor at St. Mary's.
And he was right; I was frustrated. But, now, when
I look back over the years we spent at Notre Dame,
I know the experience itself of being so closely
allied to a stimulating university was
magnificently rewarding. The discussions at
parties at Notre Dame and St. Mary's alone
provided an off-campus kind of education for those
of us who were not enrolled in the courses. And we
had not had as hard a time as many other couples
who were striving for degrees.

Thomas Schlereth's, "The University of Notre
Dame, A Portrait of its History and Campus,"
comments on one such couple: Notre Dame student
Eugene Jaeger, a father of four in 1951, commuted
two days a week to an East Chicago steel plant,
while his wife, June, worked the three-to-eleven
shift for U.S. Rubber Company in Mishawaka. When
his G.I. Bill benefits ran out, and his wife
became pregnant, Jaeger began a hectic daily
schedule: eight a.m. to noon, he worked as an
engineer at Bendix in South Bend; one p.m. to
five p.m., he attended his University classes; and
six p.m. to ten p.m., he continued his job at
Bendix. In between, says Schlereth, he studied.

"Anthony, I know we're really very lucky," I put
in. "You do have a decent job and I have my
contests."

"Your contests!" he exclaimed. "And just what

have you won lately?" he teasingly demanded to know.

Taking him by the hand, I led the way to the study and pointed. On his desk was a shiny, new, ivory-cased radio, the end result of twenty-five words on "why I prefer Motorola T.V.'s." On the wall was a black and gold modernistic thirty-five dollar clock, won in a margarine contest.

"Please," Anthony begged, "don't tell me how you won the clock!" His ears had been particularly sensitive to puns. But I couldn't resist. The margarine company had emphasized that meat fried in their brand was delicious. The contest was running through the Christmas holidays, so, my winning entry to the jingle was: "'Merry Crispness,' says the meat."

"O Lord, deliver me!" Anthony cried melodramatically.

But, he was not to be delivered. I reminded him that four hundred miles away, in Pennsylvania, was a Speed Queen automatic washing machine I had won for his Mother. And, in our garage were roller skates, a fishing rod, a tennis racquet, and a beautiful two-wheeler bike. All were won for the family during the past few months.

"Well," Anthony said, "what I meant was you haven't won any C-A-S-H! You keep saying 'I'll win cash in the next contest I enter', but you never do. Now don't misunderstand, I'm perfectly satisfied. You're doing very well, but I think you're frustrated. You've admitted you are."

There was some truth in what the gentlemen was saying. But I was satisfied in many ways.

Even if there was not a big bank account, a

Ph.D. and a Ph.T. in the house, there were four wonderful children who all showed promise. Stephanie's teacher, a nun, who apparently saw Stephanie the same way I did, described her as "the dumbest, most intelligent girl" she knew.

And just before the summer vacation had begun, I experienced a thrill that not too many mothers have had.

"Mrs. Black," said the voice on the other end of the phone, "this is the principal. I'm calling to tell you that your son, Robert, has been selected to carry the May Queen's train in the May Day procession."

"That's very nice," I commented.

"I want you to realize what a great honor this is," said the nun. "The basis on which the two boys were selected, and the only basis, was behavior. I called down over the intercom," the sister continued, "and asked the second-grade teachers to send me the best-behaved boy in each class. Robert was the one sent to me from his class."

"I'm very honored," I said.

"He will need," the principal continued, "his dark blue First Communion suit, a pair of white gloves, and," she added emphatically, "a haircut!"

"Yes, Sister," I said, obediently. (If I had confessed that I was his barber she might have rescinded his great honor.)

Then there was Mary Kay, the child of imagination. Caught up in the space age, and reflecting the newness of it all, she talked of rockets and launches and countdowns in steady conversation. How far she had traveled in her world of fantasy became apparent one warm summer afternoon when she breathlessly ran into the house shrieking: "There's a melted Martian out on the sidewalk! Go and see! Quick!" True enough, there was a yellow blob there at the curb — a quart-size jar of mayonaise Anthony had dropped moments before as he carried bags of groceries into the house!

So, if I were discouraged in the present, or "frustrated" as Anthony had termed it, there was hope for the future or at least for the future generation. Baby Bernard had, by this time, lost all his initial chubbiness and now resembled a long string bean, but he was my baby, and, fat or skinny, I loved him. So, the Ph.D. and Ph.T. could go hang and so could all the contests that ever were or ever would be.

And then the phone rang. I was upstairs with the baby, so Anthony took the message. I couldn't make out any of the words, but I thought it was good news by the tone of his voice. As I started downstairs I heard him repeating over the phone, "You'll come around in the morning to present the check!" By the time I reached the bottom step Anthony was placing the receiver in its cradle on the wall. "You did it!" he shouted. "You won FIVE HUNDRED DOLLARS in that car-battery contest you entered. The Delco dealer said that your entry stating that Delco gave you the best "spurting" chance was the one that won." Anthony was ecstatic, as was I. I had finally won C-A-S-H. Although it was four o'clock in the afternoon; it was the dawning of a new day.

Meanwhile, the British Army had run into a disturbing barrage of artillery. The research director wanted more primary source information. He also wanted to know the over-tones and the under-tones, the intrigues and the innuendoes, and of course, the facts point by point, year by year, subject by subject, and the interpretation of it all. And, incidentally, just why did the Boers favor ponies over horses in their skirmishes with the British in South Africa? To think that after five hundred pages of tedious accounting of the British and their army and it was not enough. For the time being, the Army was forced to retreat, — back to the drawing board.

Meanwhile, back in Pennsylvania, a truck had crashed into the side of our bowling alley. The driver had insurance, our manager assured us, but just what did we want to do until a contractor could be obtained? Also, when the rains came from the north, a section of the roof leaked causing damage to one of the bowling lanes. It was becoming increasingly clear that we would soon have to think about moving closer to our business enterprise. Of course, this meant leaving our beloved St. Mary's and neither of us was able to voice the words. Finally, Anthony told his superiors that he would be looking for employment with a Pennsylvania college to be near to his bowling business in the fall. Black Manor became a listing in the "For Sale" section of The South Bend Tribune.

"Are we really going to move?" Robbie wanted to know. He, more than any of the other children, regretted the change. "Gosh, how am I going to leave my gang?" he would ask.

Although Stephanie was more philosophical about
it, she was upset too about leaving St. Mary's
because she had had an active career there in
dramatics. Whenever a play called for a child's
part, Stephanie was always assured a role. "But
I'm eleven now," she said, "and I'm getting bigger
all the time. Why, I'm almost as tall as a lot of
the St. Mary's girls now." So, she realized that
her days as a child actress were numbered.

To Mary Kay and Bernard, home was where their
tricycles were parked, so, it didn't make much
difference. But to the adults in Black Manor,
changing addresses was a serious business,
especially when it involved changing the place of
employment and exchanging the Hoosier State again
for the Keystone. There were many good friends,
ideal neighbors, a bridge club, and Vetville ties
that went back ten years! Breaking away would be
exceedingly painful.

"If we're going to see to it that the children
are educated, though," Anthony reassured himself,
"we have no choice. We've got to make the bowling
business a going concern. I can't educate the kids
on my salary."

(If we had stayed at St. Mary's, educating the
girls would have been no problem since the Sisters
of Holy Cross had always had a policy of educating
daughters of faculty members, gratis. It was
years, however, before any comparable set-up was
established at Notre Dame for the sons of St.
Mary's faculty members.)

"And what about your Ph.D.?" I wanted to know.

"I can finish it in Pennsylvania," Anthony
replied. "The University of Pittsburgh's library

is near enough, the Library of Congress is closer there than here, and anything else can possibly be had from the Inter-Library loan." What he left out was a primary concern. Since he wanted to continue teaching, how was he to find time to teach classes, work in a bowling alley, and finish his dissertation?

We began to put our affairs in order and the applications went out once again. Was there any college in the Pittsburgh vicinity interested in a man who could teach English history, Western civilization, church history, Russian history, Nineteenth Century, Twentieth Century, and of course, current events?

There was. St. Vincent's College in Latrobe, Pennsylvania, needed a modern European man. St. Vincent's was the oldest Benedictine college in the country. It was also an archabbey with an archabbot in charge. And, instead of nuns and girls there would be monks and boys.

Selling the house without the aid of a real estate company was a real bother. Along with the absence of a systematic arrangement for appointments — "Saw your sign and thought we'd stop in!" — you and your housekeeping, or lack of it, was a matter of public record.

Luckily, Black Manor interested a well-known historian and prolific writer of books from Notre Dame who subsequently bought it. "I'll be able to walk to my office from here every day," declared the renowned Dr. Marshall Smelser. "This is great!"

Now, the Black family had a business and a job, but no home!

St. Vincent's College, Latrobe, PA.

When classes ended in June the problem of the moment was to make a trip to Pennsylvania to find a house. Moving day was set for late July, and the movers would have to have a place at the other end to put the furniture. At the end of a hectic week, we settled for a small, red brick, well-shrubbed house in the Borough of White Oak which we could rent.

In due time, Black Manor was given a house cooling, at which occasion, we said good-bye to all our Hoosier dear ones. Professor Black was given farewell parties and farewell cakes by his students, and Robbie said goodbye to his buddies and took one last look at his Little League field. As the Golden Dome of Notre Dame faded in the distance, we realized we were no longer a part of beautiful St. Mary's. Notre Dame, Indiana, was a thing of the past.

Once in Pennsylvania, we discovered that life did go on. On the street where we now lived, there were new friends and new playmates. St. Vincent's was an impressive college, nestled picturesquely at the foothills of the Allegheny Mountains. And, as Anthony soon discovered, the monks were amiable scholars and the boys, well, they weren't his girls, but they were "A-okay."

In between classes and lectures, the strikes and spares, the British Army was once more mustering. Important microfilm was secured through the University of Pittsburgh, and a good part of our Christmas vacation was spent in Washington, D.C., at the Library of Congress. The British Army was again taking the offensive.

There were teas for the ladies from time to time

Boniface Wimmer, Founder of St. Vincent's College

at St. Vincent's and some evenings there were excellent lectures. It was only when we longed to hear the Notre Dame band playing the Victory March or yearned for a stroll around St. Mary's Lake that we nostalgically thought of days gone by. But there was no turning back. As new leagues were obtained for the bowling lanes and our finances achieved an almost stable element, we were thankful that we had made the decision to move.

Being able to look in on Mother, also, instead of worrying about her from a distance, was a big plus. We had been good friends, and now, at last, we had the time and the opportunity to become best friends. Also, I was now only seventeen miles from my mother's only sister, Aunt Hilda, a colorful personality in the family who was called, behind her back, the Delphic Oracle. She, who had large quantities of extra-sensory-perception, had grown up in an age where anything of this nature was always dismissed, especially in Catholic circles, as "the work of the devil!"

Aunt Hilda, who was always most generous with her time and gift, would invariably wind up in the fortune-telling booth at the annual bazaar for a Pittsburgh charity, earning money for a most worthy cause, and then spend weeks afterwards trying to find an "understanding" priest — (one who would not deem her possessed) — to "confess" that she was telling fortunes again. She found one finally whom she dubbed, "the embroidery priest" because he considered her ability to "see" things as a talent, "just as being able to fashion beautiful embroidery is a gift from God," she would quote him.

Aunt Hilda would read tea leaves but much preferred coffee grounds because "they make a neater pattern." She really didn't need anything, however, to "see." Aunt Hilda's talents were all-pervasive. She just "saw."

Like the time she and Mother were in a restaurant in Atlantic City reading the menu when a waitress approached the table. Aunt Hilda looked up, saw the waitress, of course, but, oh, so much more. "My dear," she addressed the waitress, "what are all those lovely-colored fish doing around your head?"

"Hilda," my mother warned, "you're frightening her."

"They're so beautiful!" she continued. "Whatever do you do with fish?"

"I — I work in a fish cannery in the winter months," the waitress stammered, backing away from the table, uncertain she should proceed with the order.

"I see you have a son," Aunt Hilda persisted. "He's twenty-one, isn't he?"

"Twenty-two," answered the waitress feebly. "Had a birthday the other day," she mumbled.

When the food order was ready the waitress fairly threw the plates in a frantic gesture so as to stay far away from this customer who had crossed barriers no one had ever penetrated with her before. "Such an interesting life she has," Aunt Hilda clucked over her food. "It's too bad she's afraid to talk to me about it."

Mother knew that I was not afraid to talk to Aunt Hilda and she said, "Virginia, why don't you consult Aunt Hilda about whether or not Anthony is ever going to finish his Ph.D.?"

"Better yet, why not let Anthony consult her?" I suggested. From first-hand experience Anthony, a complete cynic, had come to the conclusion that there was definitely something to her gift.

Mother's respect for her sister's ESP went back to Depression days when Aunt Hilda, coming for a rare visit, had said to her, "You're putting money away, aren't you, Anne? Stashing it aside for a new furnace? And Barney (my father) doesn't know you're doing it."

Mother replied, "I don't know what you're talking about."

To which Aunt Hilda said, "I see you putting money in a box within a box. You've got about ninety-four dollars now."

Mother insisted that Aunt Hilda was far afield.

The truth of the matter was that for months, whenever an extra nickel, dime, or quarter presented itself, Mother had been saving them, but she had not counted the money, nor had she any idea of how much she had accumulated. She only knew that a new furnace was the goal. When Aunt Hilda left, however, Mother went quickly to the cedar chest in her bedroom and extracted the cardboard box. "The box within a box," she said to herself. Then she counted the contents. The sum came to exactly ninety-four dollars and forty-one cents in pennies, nickels, quarters, and half-dollars. "It was then that I became a believer," admitted Mother.

Anthony was always too busy to visit Aunt Hilda, so, when the right time presented itself, I asked her myself.

"He'll finish," she said simply, squinting up

her eyes the way she did, "but not the way you expect he will and, it won't be for a while yet. He's got to go a distance yet. He won't be able to write until he goes a distance, a far distance, but why do I keep seeing the word "Irish" through everything?" she asked.

That night, I told Anthony of Aunt Hilda's prediction and we were both baffled as to the meaning of why Aunt Hilda said, "Why do I keep seeing the word Irish?"

"Of course she saw Irish," Anthony said. "I'm getting the degree from Notre Dame, home of the Fighting Irish. I'm not even a warlock, and I know that!" The implication had been noticed.

"Well, she said you'd finish and that's encouraging, I tried to brighten up the conversation.

Just as we were beginning to get our bearings in Pennsylvania somewhat and feel as though we just might belong after all, a startling request via the telephone shattered our temporary tranquility. The owner of our house in White Oak had been transferred back to the area! Could he please have his house back, and, yes, he knew the lease said we had six months yet on it, but, maybe, if we looked around — we could find something sooner. After all, why wait to make a move you know is inevitable?

And the want ads were pursued again.

In South Bend, Black Manor had five bedrooms! But finding four bedrooms in Pennsylvania was proving to be our bugaboo. We would settle for three, then, but houses for rent were so few. And we couldn't swing buying one just yet.

It was the time of the year when the first-graders were being registered in the schools. Where could I register Mary Kay, who had been six years of age in March, when I had no idea in which locality we would be living? I decided to register her, temporarily, perhaps, in the spanking-new Catholic school in White Oak, — St. Angela's.

"But, Sister," I said to the tall, attractive Sister of St. Joseph who was the principal of St. Angela's, "I do not know what our address will be in the fall. We have to move . . .," and I told her my story.

"You need a house," she said simply. "Here," she said, reaching into her desk drawer for a tiny statue of St. Joseph. "Pray to St. Joseph. Tell him your troubles. He'll see to it that God finds you a house."

Back home, I placed the tiny carving on Anthony's chest of drawers and then promptly forgot all about it. But, I was to find out three days later, St. Joseph is one saint who is not to be ignored!

"This ad sounds all right," said Anthony the next evening as he read the Daily News. "I'll mark it. Please try to call the realty company early in the morning," he instructed.

But the next morning I had forgotten all about everything except that Bernard was to get his final polio shot and Mary Kay was in line for a tooth-cleaning. Since the following day was Saturday, Anthony called about the ad.

"Come right over," the man on the phone instructed. "The caretaker for the church will show you around." It was not until we saw the lay of the land that we realized that the house for rent was the parsonage of the Central Presbyterian Church in McKeesport, Pennsylvania.

"But why isn't your minister living here?" we asked.

"The present minister has one child," the man replied. "This place is simply too big. The church rents a little house in White Oak for him."

Once inside the large, red brick, ivy-covered manse, as the caretaker called it, we understood what he meant. The living room was the size of a ballroom, the dining room a miniature skating rink, and the kitchen a gymnasium. And so beautiful! The ad had said four bedrooms, but it failed to say that three additional rooms on the third floor could easily be used as bedrooms. This beautiful, newly-painted, well-landscaped, four-bedroom home, with two powder rooms in addition to the master bathroom, was available for approximately the same amount of rent we had been paying for our present house.

I carefully avoided getting my hopes up. After all, the house was a parsonage, connected in various ways in addition to paths and sidewalks, to a church of which we were not members. Perhaps, the Elders would be saving it for one of their own members. We thanked the caretaker and immediately called the man at the realty company.

"Stop in on Monday," he said, "to fill out an application."

On Monday afternoon, we learned that our application would have to be approved by all members of the church board. The entire church board of Elders would have to say "yes."

"We'll never make it," I said over and over.

"If Kennedy made it into the White House," Anthony said wryly, "we might make it into the Presbyterian Parsonage."

Tuesday afternoon we had the word. "Move right in," the head of the board told us. "Glad to have you!"

"I can't believe it!" I said exuberantly. "I can't believe we made it! And, come to think of it, I never said 'beans' to St. Joseph!" Nary one syllable passed my lips in petition for Joseph's intercession, and here we had a house anyway.

I relayed this information to the Sister of St. Joseph when I called to tell her that Mary Kay would not be attending St. Angela's because we were territorially in St. Pius V parish boundaries.

"No, dear," she answered sweetly. "You didn't say 'beans' to St. Joseph. But you must remember, my dear, that I did!" The put-down of the entire generation, and the making of a believer! I replaced the receiver, transformed!

"St. Joseph," I apologized, "I believe. Help my unbelief!"

The height, length and depth of the manse was invigorating. Although there were times when I felt spread all over the place, like an octopus whose tentacles were out in every direction, I mostly enjoyed the sweeping quality of the old house. While wiping up a floor here, or cleaning out a closet there, I would quietly remind myself to do it well. It might by years before I would be able to get back to it!

The day when Professor Black discovered that

each time the lawn of the Central Presbyterian Church was cut, the parsonage's grass was clipped, too, was a glorious one. "It's what I've always wanted," he confided, "my own private gardener."

The secretary at the church was most friendly and helpful. And there was George, the caretaker, who could do all sorts of odd jobs. But over everything, reigning supreme, were the pigeons. Cooing or flapping, the pigeons were always fascinating. Here was St. Mark's Square as well as Trafalgar! To look out the kitchen window, or any of the fifty-odd windows of the house, and see them soaring among the church's pinnacles and towers was exhilarating! And, to look up suddenly and discover that a stray pigeon was watching you at your work from a nearby ledge, was a new kind of challenge!

Stephanie shared my aviary interest and claimed one of the third-floor rooms as her own private 'bird room' complete with binoculars, a primitive microscope, nature books and an Audubon Bird Guide.

The pigeon, like the dove, is a symbol of peace according to books that carry such information. And, the Professor and I were finding peace there, in our Presbyterian Manse. The Presbyterians were extremely tolerant of the "Mickeys" who lived on their premises. When I did my dishes, humming "Holy, Holy, Holy" along with their congregation, I felt as though the whole ecumenical movement was gathering momentum. Invariably, when the Blacks would be going to Mass on Sunday mornings with their Roman missals tucked under their arms, they would meet the Protestant church-goers coming from their ten o'clock service. Friendliness always prevailed.

I will admit that I did try to make the impression that I was taking good care of their parsonage. The cleaning lady at the Church, an Irish Catholic, cheered our occupancy of the manse with encouraging words:

"You're safe for the time being," she informed, "as long as a very elderly minister doesn't come, or a young assistant minister with a large family." The elderly man would prefer living on top of the church. The young minister would need the big house for his family. But, when after one year, none of these things happened, we heaved a sigh and renewed our lease.

We had learned much in a year's time. We learned that if the children, the little ones, went out on the porch early on Sunday morning, they invariably received nickels and dimes from haphazard churchgoers who did not know that the minister was no longer in residence at the parsonage. We learned, too, that as long as some people mistook us for the minister or minister's wife, our credit was extremely good.

"Don't bother yourself about running up those steps for the money now," the bread man used to say. "Spare yourself." I did. Sometimes a bill would come to five loaves of bread in five days, and I would pay on the sixth. But, then one day I was asked a question: "How was church attendance last Sunday?" When I explained that I really didn't know, credit suddenly disappeared.

While the new mistress of the manse could deal with the bread-men and salesmen, there was one category, — those looking for a hand-out "from the parson," that proved to be extremely difficult.

It was the Methodist minister, one block away, who coached me on how to deal with these "charity" cases. He had cautioned from the beginning, "Don't bother with any of them." But I had no intention of following his advice. After all, if a man is hungry, I would have to feed him, wouldn't I?

"Beware," he said, "if it's money they want. It will be a drink that they're after. I've been taken many times. I have even gone to the grocery store with these men, bought their groceries, paid the bill — only to find out later that they hocked the food and bought drink. It's a shame that some of these rummies are in the habit of coming to the parsonage. Call your minister if you're bothered, and if he's not home, try me. You shouldn't be expected to help. We are."

When, on one excruciatingly hot day in July, a middle-aged man of ruddy complexion appeared in the doorway asking for the parson, I felt I had been primed for the occasion. He was looking for work; he came all the way from Monessen, Pennsylvania, and he needed a job desperately.

"But, why come to McKeesport?" I asked. "This is a depressed area now. Many are unemployed here."

"May I please have a drink of water?" he responded quietly.

I asked him to remain on the porch while I got it. Three glasses of lemonade later, he confided that he had previously been everywhere but McKeesport looking for work. After half a box of graham crackers, I learned he was not married, but that he was the sole support of his elderly parents.

After many phone calls to the Presbyterian minister in White Oak, who, I finally realized, had left town for a short while, I called my own pastor who was also away. I then called my Methodist minister friend.

"Tell him to go to the Salvation Army if he needs a bed for the night," he advised.

"He says he was there already and that the beds aren't clean."

"Listen," the minister cautioned, "you'll eat and sleep in dirt if you're really poor. But that's not true, the Salvation Army quarters are really clean. I've been there many times. This guy sounds like a swindler. Did he get any money from you?"

"No," I answered.

"Good," replied the minister. "Keep it that way. Tell him to go to the Salvation Army. They'll help him from there. Nobody comes here from Monessen looking for work. Only if they really don't want to find any. I think you've got a rummy on your hands and I'm sorry again that you have to be bothered." That was the end of the conversation. He would have run over but he had an afternoon wedding ceremony to perform.

"I'll pack you a supper," I told the man on the porch, "and tell you how to get to the Salvation Army. That's all I can do." The man took out a large handkerchief and wiped his brow. The Salvation Army Headquarters was quite a distance. Perhaps, I should give him a bus token to get there. That wasn't money, just a bus token. He looked so broken, sitting there on the step.

I handed the lunch and bus token to him. His eyes moistened in gratitude as he asked for one more favor. He was terribly worried about his parents. They were deaf, so he couldn't phone them. He had been gone three days now looking for work. He really should be going home but the bus fare was one dollar and seventy-five cents, and all he had was the bus token.

As I shook the last nickel from Mary Kay's doggie-bank, I was convinced I was doing the right thing. The Methodist minister hadn't seen this man. After all, this one was really worried about his parents, and one dollar and seventy-five cents wouldn't make or break us.

When the man had finally gone I found myself humming: "Whatsoever you do to the least of my brethren, that you do unto Me . . .," But just to quiet that tiny, almost completely hidden qualm, I dialed the bus terminal.

"What is the bus fare from McKeesport to Monessen?" I asked the terminal's spokesman.

"Three dollars and sixty-eight cents," the voice replied.

"Are you sure?" I asked. She was sure.

And so was I. So was I.

Thirty Miles from Pittsburgh lies Seton Hill College nestled in the hills of Greensburg, PA.

IX
Hazard Yet Forward! Seton Hill

One evening, a telephone call diverted our plan of action completely. The call was for Anthony, and its request startled him. Would he consider a position of assistant professor of history at Seton Hill College? True, he had applied there before leaving St. Mary's, but there had been no opening at that time, and St. Vincent's had hired him. Now he was at St. Vincent's and enjoyed working with the faculty and students.

But Seton Hill's offer was tempting. Seton Hill was my alma mater, a solid academic stronghold situated on a high hill overlooking Greensburg, Pennsylvania, and, like St. Vincent's, located in the foothills of the Allegheny Mountains. Seton Hill was closer to our bowling alley than was St. Vincent's, and Seton Hill's students happened to be girls. Girls and nuns — the Professor could be back in his old, familiar environment that he had grown so fond of while at St. Mary's.

"My girls," Anthony used to say, "will make wonderful history teachers." (I hadn't heard him say that about any of "his boys" at St. Vincent's.)

"Go where you would most benefit your family,"

175

the deeply spiritual, scientist-president of St. Vincent's advised Anthony. And he added, "Truly, our budget cannot afford to top Seton Hill's offer. But don't worry, St. Vincent's will find a replacement before the fall term."

"Hazard Yet Forward!" The Seton Hill motto on its coat of arms sprung to mind. Seton Hill held the promise of many interesting things to come, — garden parties, traditional big-sister, little-sister faculty get-togethers, first-rate lectures, skiing parties to the nearby mountains — things I had known first hand. Yes, Seton Hill would be fine for the Professor and also his family.

"Hazard yet forward — ever onward!" was Seton Hill's cry; red and gold its colors, with the delightful Sisters of Charity steering its course. The Sister's Foundress, Mother Elizabeth Ann Seton, was beatified then. Many classes began with: "Let us offer this prayer that Elizabeth Ann Seton will be canonized a saint." And secretly I thought: "She'll never make it. We've been praying an eternity!" But, I was happy Elizabeth Seton was canonized in 1975 and I was proved wrong.

Seton Hill. The name itself had a good sound to it. I laughed to myself when I recalled the recent words of Mother Victoria when she spied the Black family walking across the Seton Hill campus. "My dear," she said, addressing me. "When you were here at Seton Hill I thought that someday you would join our community and become a Sister of Charity." Then her eyes moved slowly to Anthony, then to Stephanie, who was standing beside me, then to Robbie, then to Mary Kay, and finally to little Bernard. "But," she added, smiling her

"Hazard Yet Forward" - Motto of Seton Hill over door of the
Athletic building.

Seton Hill College, Greensburg, PA.

Athletic Building - Seton Hill College.

mystical smile and shaking her head, "I don't want you now."

A few more phone calls, a few interviews and it was all settled. Come fall, the Professor would be back with his girls! Come fall, the bowling leagues would again form and throw their balls down the alleys and their money into the cash register. Come fall, the mum plants would be blooming at the Presbyterian Parsonage and the pigeons would be soaring on high as usual. Then come winter, the bowling season would reach its peak.

But, this winter . . . this winter would be different from all previous winters. This winter, icy, steel fingers of grief would seek out the earth's very heart and freeze it!

When the maple leaves in Mother's backyard flushed their first tippets of red in late October, malignant cancer cells were even then increasing within her. And, when the maple leaves had long been buried beneath the indiscriminating snows of stark January, Mother's illness terminated in death. In the ninety-odd days she was confined to bed, love between mother and daughter flourished anew, opening and surrendering itself ultimately to that mysterious separation — death.

I marvelled that there had been no pain. Cancer of the pancreas is known to be quick and relatively painless. "Is she suffering now?" I asked the doctor who came to give Mother the first, last and only shot she had had in the entire three months I cared for her.

"Do you think she is?" he asked me.

"No," I answered.

"She's dying," he said simply. "She's not suffering."

Snow fell that January 13th and continued to fall into January 14th, and, providentially, prevented my going home to the parsonage to get supper for Anthony and the children. Home was only three miles away, but with the snow measuring twenty inches and no end in sight, travelling was an impossibility. I gratefully depended on Anthony's mother and sisters to take over, and, therefore, knowing that this part of my family was safe and warm for the moment, I could concentrate on Mother and the final moments. In this, I was joined by my sister Rita, who, being widowed the year before, made her home with Mother.

And still the snow fell, and gradually, Mother stopped calling our names and slept peacefully, intermittently, and the winterness and starkness of the night penetrated all living things. In the soft light up in the blue bedroom Mother was breathing slowly and surely, but then little gaps in between slipped through ever so gradually. Then the pauses between the risings and the fallings grew longer and longer, and suddenly, my sister and I knelt transfixed at mysterious death.

At 1:30 a.m., January 14, 1964, death came into the pretty blue bedroom, and even though it wrought such a drastic change, it left the bedroom still pretty. The soft lights were still shining, but Mother was gone. Death had been quiet — very quiet. It had even been serene, but most of all, it had been so very natural. Like it was the most ordinary thing that anyone could ever do.

182

"I'll miss that valiant spirit," my sister said quietly.

"The surgeon, who said that Mother would live only three months, had been right all along," I thought in the abject stillness of the room. Mother's illness took precisely three months and three days. And, even with cancer, she did not suffer. I was grateful.

Mother had lived and died, and now she had died to live. She had come full circle. I was happy for her, but devastated for myself. I had lost my best friend and the days ahead would be devoid of participatory living. Going through the motions was all I could do. A body could continue making omelets and beds in a frozen, mechanical way, but a grieving member of society could be expected to function only at half mast when it came time for deciding whether or not a trip to Pittsburgh every Saturday morning should be undertaken for a class for Stephanie in the dramatic arts, · or whether braces were in order for Robbie's teeth or should be postponed until he was older since his teeth were still 'moving'. There were times when instead of making beds, I simply crawled into them. Was my inability to cope the reason that Bernard was having so many problems adjusting to kindergarten? Getting number four through college would be a simple matter compared to the complicated maze kindergarten was proving to be.

"Why not hold him back a year?" I proposed to the teacher.

"He may be your baby at home," she informed me, "but he gets his work in school and there's no reason to keep him back. He's very sensitive," she added, "and cries a lot."

In spite of all lessons on dressing himself, however, Bernard would frequently come home from school looking like the Hunchback of Notre Dame with his little sweater in a roll on his back, with tears brimming in his eyes.

"How's Bernard doing?" Anthony asked from behind his evening newspaper when I returned from the school's Open House Night.

"His school work's fine," I replied, talking to the paper, "but the teacher thinks we should take him to a psychiatrist!"

The newspaper lowered inch by inch. Incredulity shone from Anthony's eyes. "In the name of God," he stated solemnly, "he's the only normal kid we've had!"

I agreed, but I knew that because I was still grieving, the times were still abnormal. Fortunately, however, life and living began taking on a permanency of sorts with the friendliness exhibited by the Seton Hill faculty. Mother's happy face and happy laugh were gone, but the memories were all good ones. The familiarity of returning now and then to Seton Hill helped fill the tremendous void. The Seton Hill people included our family in many functions. In fact, we were attending a party in honor of a Seton Hill colleague the night of the wind — the night the tornado hit.

"It's gone, — gone with the wind," Anthony's sister reported to us via the telephone. "Four people have called us and said so," she added.

"It's the roof of the bowling alley," Anthony told me quietly. "It's been blown off. Everyone is all right, though. No one is hurt, but we had better go see what we can do."

Enroute, the car radio informed us that another roof in the area, that of the Glassport skating rink, had collapsed on one thousand skaters. "That rink couldn't hold more than two hundred people," Anthony said, while driving through the steady downpour.

The radio announcer also reported that two of the known dead from the storm had been in a Glassport hotel that had fallen into its own cellar! A state of emergency was declared. No one could enter the area without official sanction. Electric wires were down everywhere.

"How will we get in?" I wanted to know.

"I don't know," Anthony replied, still driving through torrents of thrashing rain.

"Where will we go from here?" I asked myself. In the words of Mary Kay, which we were to learn later, "the only reason my Daddy left South Bend was to look after his business. Now, — Ph-h-h-h-h-h-h-h-h-h-h-h-t! It's all blown away!"

At the Glassport city limits we were told we could not enter because there was too much obstruction in the way. "Try going over the hill," the tired-looking officer told us. "This way, along the river, is out."

It was 1:00 a.m. when we entered the dead city of Glassport, Pennsylvania, population nine thousand, birthplace of my parents and myself. Black somberness was everywhere. The only light in the entire town was a gas light, proudly flickering in front of the Peoples' Natural Gas Company. We slowly picked our way through the rubble. Trees were uprooted, glass and bricks filled the streets. Cars were leveled to the ground, some with concrete blocks still perched atop their remains. Buildings were battered beyond recognition. Portable spotlights now began playing on the wreckage. Steam shovels were digging at the hotel rubble looking for more victims.

"How many customers were there at the bar? Did you notice any strangers?" The volunteers kept asking while digging.

A passerby told us, "There were only twenty-three skaters in the rink. Some were hurt. But no two hundred were in it when it collapsed. And no one thousand, as the radio announcer had said. Thank God!"

With only a packet of matches and a flickering flashlight, we made our way finally to the bowling alley. What greeted our eyes was a bowling business that had an intact roof — all but for one section. The north-west corner of the roof was gone. "The saints be praised!" I echoed my Irish Grandmother. But inside, water damage had taken its toll. The lanes were covered with water; water filled the gutters of the bowling lanes; water was already warping the highly-polished, sleek, maple wood that framed the alleys. Still dressed in our party clothes, we set to work mopping, soaking up the water in every which way, until the sun started its climb in the east.

"We aren't wiped out," I said, when we finally stopped for tea.

"No, we were lucky," Anthony agreed, "and hopefully our insurance will cover most of the damage because all of the lanes will have to be reconditioned."

Hand in hand, we slowly and thankfully made our

way tediously to the car, pausing to stand aghast
at the number of homes and businesses, factory
buildings, gasoline stations and schools that
stood windowless, roofless, some completely
unrecognizable! Hours later, ambulances were still
carrying the injured to hospitals while for
others, burial arrangements were being made. The
damage estimate in dollars and cents, — seven
million dollars, came days later.

As we drove home to our parsonage, still in our
crumpled glad-sad rags, we realized we were very
lucky people. Our kids were happy and healthy. The
tornado hadn't even come close to our home.

But, perhaps, we had thanked our lucky stars too
soon, because the very next day's mail contained a
letter from the research director at Notre Dame
concerning Anthony's dissertation.

The director said that he had been giving the
British Army a lot of thought lately. There was
much, no doubt, that could be salvaged from
Anthony's six hundred pages of research. But, as
he saw it, the subject was just too broad. The
British Army, 1902-1914, was unwieldly, he said.
Perhaps it might be better if Anthony could find a
new subject. Wasn't he tired of this one, anyway?
Hadn't it gone stale after all these years? A new
subject, with new research, might be just what the
ticket needed to gain the freshness and singleness
of purpose so necessary in writing a dissertation.
What was needed was one crystallized, structurized
ladder to a well-defined analysis. This mountain
of subject matter had to go!

It was crisis time again for the Black family.
We all wanted to say things like: "We don't care

if you never get a Ph.D. What difference does it
make if you never get a thesis finished? We love
you." But of course we didn't say anything.
Because he cared. And because it did matter.

The response of the children to the staggering
setback reminded me of the way we had all acted
when Bernard had made an airplane in woodworking
while he was still in kindergarten. The teacher
apparently said something to him about the fact
that his airplane didn't look much like an
airplane.

To Bernard's inconsolable sobs everyone
exclaimed, "We don't care if your airplane doesn't
look much like an airplane! Maybe that teacher
never saw that kind of airplane before because
it's a new invention! So what if your airplane
doesn't look like other airplanes? We like it that
way."

As we did with Bernard, we wanted to gather the
Professor in our collective arms and tell him that
it didn't matter about his airplane.

"You won't get your Ph.T.," he finally said.
"And its all my fault. If I don't get my Ph.D.,
you don't get anything either."

How do you convince a guy that when you've got
everything you don't need anything? "I've already
got my Ph.T.," I replied.

"Oh?" said Anthony.

"Yes," I said. "My Philosophy Degree in Trauma
— the Ph.T. . . ." I proudly stated, moving
adroitly away from target range. But it was hard
to laugh when a world you had been building for
fifteen years had just dissolved to dust.

The blow had fallen. The British Army was in

final retreat. With the exception of the chapters on compulsory military training (style 1914), which could possibly be worked into timely articles, the entire six hundred pages could be now filed in our own private Dead Letter Office.

"How do I start over again, at my age?" Anthony asked his mother.

To which she replied, "One door never closes, but that another opens up." But where was this other door?

Fortunately, we had too many obligations and kids to wallow in our dilemma. Anthony immersed himself in his teaching, realizing that without a Ph.D. degree, his future as an historian would be limited. He compensated by trying to develop new incentives, new business expertise to entice leagues to enroll at our bowling alley.

Meanwhile, I busied myself in housecleaning, made minor repairs at home, involved myself in contests once more, and put my name on the substitute teaching list. Privately we both wondered and worried if an extension in time would be granted Anthony by Notre Dame for his Ph.D. dissertation.

One Monday morning, my worries were put aside in that I was called to fill in for a teacher who was in the process of having a nervous breakdown. As I learned later, the trouble with the class was primarily that it was part of an educational experiment. Of the five third-grade classes in the school, this one was the one that tallied the most children with low I.Q.'s. It also contained several emotionally disturbed children and was comprised of mostly over-aged boys for that grade level. Instead of weeks, as originally anticipated, I would spend months working with these little ones.

My class, it seemed, was always in a wrestling heap. Clenching my teeth, I would wade through bodies and kicking legs until I thought I had exhumed the deepest and innermost core-bound trouble-maker. I would then try for arbitration. No matter what the strategy, however, a conflagration always broke out anew, and the accusations would follow:

"He poked me first."

"Did not. He stuck his finger in my eye," and then the denial.

My class's conversations were to the point: "We're gonna move again 'cause the rent is due."

"Me and my brother saw that movie five times. We hid under the seats so the usher couldn't see us."

"I was late for school because my momma was drinkin' last night and didn't get up soon enough."

Of the twenty-seven children in the class, Rubystine, an eight-year-old peace-maker, was my mainstay. A Mahalia Jackson in miniature, Ruby was the only one in the class who regularly attended church and Sunday school. Because she could belt out "He's Got the Whole World, in His Hands" and could tell the class what the minister had said the previous Sunday, she was a tremendous asset. The class was always eager to hear what Ruby had to say. When discipline would be deteriorating, I would call Ruby to the front of the class and she would calm them, interest them, sing to them, challenge them, cajole them.

"I guess the Supreme Court said we can't pray together in school," she'd say to the class, "but I guess we can sing together," and Ruby would lead them in a Sunday school song.

The day came when high winds blew at dismissal time and the principal announced over the intercom that students would remain for an indefinite period and not go home until they had subsided. An hysterical Leon jumped to his feet and shouted that nobody, nobody would keep him in school if he wanted to go home. And Rubystine calmly rose from her desk, walked to the front of the room, and spoke to her peers about how the principal knew they all wore nice hats and wouldn't want them blown away. Then, spying the open window at ceiling level (it was a basement classroom) she concluded, "Now, we'll all watch and when that little ol' wind comes in the window there, we'll open the closet door and it will go in the closet and we'll shut the door on it and keep it locked in the closet and then we can all go home."

Leon, perfectly satisfied by her words, spent the next ten minutes watching the wind's antics outside until the principal decided it was safe for everyone to leave the building.

Only once did Rubystine's choice of subject, taken from Sunday school, seem to be unwise. Before I was aware of what was coming she said in haunting tones, "You gotta be good. Take out the trash when you're told to. Scrub your teeth. Say your prayers. Dry the dishes. Take care of your baby brother or sister. Do what you're told. Listen to the teacher. Listen to the principal. 'Cause someday you'll hear a-knockin' at the door.

And you'll say, 'Who's there? Who's knockin' at my door?' And then the answer will come, slowly, quietly, 'Death is at your door. Death has come for you'!" And Ruby's pointer-finger, suddenly, was unleashed onto the class.

"No! No!" Leon was on his feet, shouting. "Not me! Not me!"

It was several minutes before order was restored, and Ruby admitted that she never heard in Sunday school that death would come "a-knockin' at the door!" She had heard only that it would come.

While Ruby was a joy to the class, Howey was an ominous threat. "I like to twist pigeon necks," he confided to me. "I creep up on 'em, when the pigeons ain't flyin'," he animatedly demonstrated, "and I try to keep ahold of the head. Then I swing 'em around like this 'til I hear the neck snap." Then he smiled a delicious smile, "That's a real sound."

Aghast, I promptly reported this conversation to the school psychologist, but no one could help Howey. By the time he was in fifth grade he had threatened the life of a teacher and also several of his classmates. And, by the time Howey was in sixth grade he was dismissed from school as a dangerous threat to other pupils.

But Howey wasn't the only one to worry about. During the course of one single school day the grocer from the corner came to visit because one of the boys had stolen a few items, a social worker came because a class member's textbooks were found on the bank of the river and he wondered if the student had drowned, and a fireman appeared who suspected one of my charges or turning in three false fire-alarms.

Arriving home I was greeted by a distressed Mary Kay who announced, "I was naughty in school today and had to stay afterwards."

I had to sit down as I asked, "What happened?"

"Well," she said, "I put my foot in the aisle and that's breaking the rule. So, Sister said I had to stay after school."

Since my pupils would just as soon walk on the top of the desks as sit in them, I did not understand. "Did you try to trip someone with your foot in the aisle?"

"Oh, no," she said, "I just forgot. I broke the rule."

"Well, Mary Kay," I found myself saying aloud. "If Sister says you should not put your foot in the aisle, and that's the rule of the classroom, then you had better remember not to put your foot in the aisle."

"Oh, the fortunate woman," I thought, "to have such a discipline problem!"

Meanwhile, as the weeks and months went by, it was evident that a neighborhood bowling business that had no automatic pinsetters nor liquor license was destined to have dwindling receipts, and, as warm weather advanced, bowling receipts retreated even farther.

When things seemed their darkest, however, the door of opportunity opened. A friend and colleague of Anthony's from Notre Dame's history department made an important suggestion. "Anthony, there's a diary, the Cavendish Irish Parliamentary Diary, that's crying for someone to edit it. It's all primary source stuff. Why don't you consider tackling it? It's a natural for a dissertation."

Anthony considered the proposal carefully. True, the subject was narrow enough, — the Irish Parliament. The years involved were only two, 1774-1776, and not fourteen as had been the case with the British Army. But, would the history department chairman grant the extension and give the green light on this subject?

"Hope springs eternal . . .," I quoted to myself . . . and our hopes were fulfilled when approval was given that same week. For what ultimately became, "AN EDITION OF THE CAVENDISH DIARY, 1774-1776," Anthony's historical contribution to Irish History was begun that very week, and by the time it was finished it consisted of thirteen hundred pages in three volumes!

Anthony and I now realized what Aunt Hilda "saw" when she looked into the future and said . . . "It will be a long time yet before Anthony gets his Ph.D., but why do I see the word Irish?"

Inscription above the east entrance archway of
Sacred Heart Church.
Photo by David F. Weber, Notre Dame '61

X

Back Home Again in Indiana

Although the Cavendish diary was in the Library
of Congress in Washington, D.C., Notre Dame also
had a copy from which Anthony was free to work. A
new research director was assigned, new beginnings
were made and all the same things Anthony and I
had said before about the aborted British Army
dissertation were said again for the Cavendish
diary:

"The writing of a dissertation is like making a
mosaic, just a few pieces a day, but someday, the
picture will be complete. We will take each day as
it comes and do a little each day."

As Anthony immersed himself in the diary he
turned more and more responsibility for the
bowling alley over to the manager and blocked in
more time for the Irish Parliament. As I proof-
read and typed Anthony's notes the abject dryness
of it all was an absolute penance. The arguments
on the floor of the Parliament were endless and
they never seemed to go anywhere. Lord So and So
wanted to increase So and So's pension to one more
pound and spent fifteen pages saying why this was
necessary. Or, the Privy Counselor had this or
that to say about some trifling. I found myself

thinking, "Who the heck cares?" time and time again. But this was a non-historical thought.

From my point of view, only about thirty pages of the entire thirteen hundred paged dissertation proved interesting. These had to do with whether or not the Irish would be asked to serve in the British Army during the American Revolution. Parliament argued pro and con, and finally, when four thousand Irish troops were dispatched to aid the harassed British Army of General Gage in Boston, intrigue in the diary quickened.

"You are putting an Army into the hands of the British Ministry to butcher your fellow subjects," one member remonstrated. Then (and only then) I chewed my gum vigorously.

Anthony, sensing my disinterest in the topic, gradually took over the typing and even the proofreading, relieving me of the drudgery.

As time went on, the fact that four hundred and ten miles separated Anthony from his new research director at Notre Dame began to annoy him. In addition, the parsonage (our home) was thirty miles from his job at Seton Hill. Add to this the frequent eight hundred mile weekend trips to Indiana and back and soon Anthony said, "I wonder if I could get my old job back at St. Mary's. It would be much easier if I were closer to the archives and closer to my director."

"But what about Seton Hill?" I asked. "Can the administration there get someone to replace you?"

Anthony replied, "There are plenty of young history professors floating around, many of whom have Ph.D.'s."

"But what about the bowling alley?" I asked.

And he replied, "The manager we have is extremely competent and honest. I'm sure he would appreciate a raise in pay to take on a little bit of added responsibility."

What we could not know at this time was that the complete unravelling of the bowling alley would take place two years hence. Located in a declining area to begin with, it simply could not compete with the many new developments in the bowling business. The lack of parking facilities and automatic pinsetting machines were its biggest drawbacks. The business, therefore, continued to lose trade year after year until the point was finally reached when the manager could not meet expenses from business revenues, and, therefore, had to close it. But this was still in the future.

When we voiced our thoughts about moving back to Notre Dame to the secretary at the Presbyterian church we learned that the Elders' plans for the parsonage (in the very near future) included its demolition for a church parking lot. The Presbyterians had been worried about telling us that we were going to have to move. So, our way was clear when the good news came that not only could Anthony return to St. Mary's and to his girls, but the librarian, Sister Rita Claire, C.S.C., would furnish him with a special room on the second floor to house his books and papers so that he could make undisturbed lightning progress on his dissertation.

The movers were called. Into the truck went all our bulky worldly goods. Then with a car load of kids and the remaining miscellany we were off, westward ho! The Pennsylvania Turnpike, then the

Ohio Toll Road, the Indiana Toll Road, and finally, home.

Home in Indiana was now a rented, white, stucco house situated on the one and only hill in South Bend overlooking a pleasant playground. It was near to the University of Notre Dame and to St. Mary's as well. Located on a large lot speckled with big maple trees, its only drawback was a slanting roof that cut off needed height in the upstairs bedrooms. Each time the owner collected the rent he would say, "See, you're getting used to those slanted bedroom ceilings, aren't you? What did I tell you?"

It was a nice house, but we did need more space, and although rentals were difficult to find, we had a goal — to walk upright in our bedrooms.

Months later we found a large, grey stone house, two miles from St. Mary's. The house was not for sale, but the rent was reasonable. We counted forty oak trees in a large, lumbering yard, and plenty of blue jays. Here, indeed, was a house in which we could be comfortable.

It had a large living room with a fireplace — the better to hang Christmas stockings on. A lovely patio — the better for Stephanie to direct all her dramatic endeavors on. A gloomy garage — the better for Robbie to produce his spook houses in. There was a sound-proof basement — the better for Mary Kay to play her clarinet in! And there was one window in Bernard's room which offered a magnificent cross-section of a wasp's hive — the better to study the goings on inside a wasp's nest, which interested everyone in the family.

And soon, I found a full-time job at John Adams

Heisman Trophy winner JOHN HUARTE with Bernard and Mary Kay.

High School in South Bend, Indiana, whose students were eager to learn.

The Cavendish Diary was being prodded, pummelled and poked into shape by Assistant Professor Anthony R. Black, who spent every extra minute editing and making scholarly notations. From his nook in the St. Mary's library, the dissertation was progressing, as were my students in Developmental Reading and Sophomore English II at John Adams, as they waded through Shakespeare's "Julius Caesar" and mastered the technique of reading with a shadow-scope. Yes, the professor was progressing, the students were progressing, and even the newest teacher at John Adams, was progressing.

The mere six hundred pages devoted to the British Army had been but a "wetting of the whistle" so to speak as one studied the loquaciousness of the Irish Parliament. The Cavendish diary was, with all verbosity, gradually turning into a gusher of the first magnitude, with eleven hundred pages having been reached and the end not yet in sight. But only the history muse could adequately ascertain how many more pages would yet be needed to fulfill Anthony's requirement for his Ph.D. And, luckily for us, the new research director was outlining the confines very carefully.

As for my Ph.T., bringing home a paycheck from a full-time teaching job was exhilarating, and teaching high school English classes, which is what I had been originally trained for, was challenging.

The students asked many questions and I

explained, "I can teach you only as much as you'll let me teach. If you are open you will learn much. If you are closed, you will learn very little. I respect you. You are a human being. There has never been anyone like you before and there will never be another like you in the future because you are an unrepeatable person with a special pattern all your own. Your finger-prints are like no other finger-prints in the universe. In the Judean-Christian tradition you are made in the image and likeness of God. This is a profound concept, one that I accept, revere and practice in my classroom."

By carefully following the syllabus, things went well enough until the day demonstration speeches were called for.

"Mrs. Black," the principal said to me in his toleratingly-best tone, "the next time you assign demonstration speeches to those characters you have fifth hour, let me know ahead of time. When the sheriff called me and said that he had picked up three of your students carrying rifles heading towards our school, we could not be expected to know that they were only bringing guns for demonstration speeches — that this was their English assignment for the day. Next time, just give me a little notice so that I can inform the law enforcement community to be ready. And, next time, do check on what they plan to be demonstrating and guide them a bit in their choices. You'll do that now, won't you? Also," the principal continued, "teaching vocabulary by means of pantomime might be a valid teaching technique to some people, but words like "cavalry," perhaps, should be eliminated from your list. You see, it is very difficult for me to explain to the superintendent why hordes of students are galloping around your classroom yelling — 'Charge!' If you could find another way — a quieter way — of getting this vocabulary business across it would be appreciated."

I promised.

*　　　*　　　*　　　*

The day we had waited for eighteen years finally dawned, June 1, 1969. The sun came up with a bouncing, bursting lilt. It was graduation day.

Relatives from Pennsylvania were arriving! There was Anthony's mother, his sisters, Loy and Patsy, and Aunt Laura, Uncle Pete, Aunt Flo, Uncle Ray, Aunt Mercedes and Uncle John. Cousins Ann and Ray lived in South Bend, so they were already on hand. My sister Mary Frances with husband, Jim, arrived from Ohio.

The cake, from the Dainty Maid Bakeshop stood ready with a mock diploma perched ceremoniously atop icing that was sinking two millimeters per hour into the cake. The champagne was standing by in the refrigerator next to the Dutch potato salad with the homemade dressing.

At 12:00 noon the bells in Sacred Heart Church on the campus of Notre Dame sang their hearts out, and all the prayers offered by the Black family were prayers of thanksgiving. In this we were joined by the students, the faculty members, and the parishioners who went before us — who whispered similiar thank-you's in the church that had served the Notre Dame community since 1852.

The Sisters of Holy Cross at St. Mary's, jubilant that their Mr. Black had finally crossed his hurdle, gave shelter to Anthony's aunt, Sister Norbertine, R.S.M., a Sister of Mercy from Pittsburgh who came for the festivities. This precipitated a thorough tour of the St. Mary's campus from Anthony's office to the heavenly-blue mosaics in the Church of Loretto.

"There are twelve hundred and fifty acres and one hundred buildings on the Notre Dame campus," Anthony said to his Uncle Pete, "which do you want to cover?"

The Lady on the Golden Dome, atop the Administration Building, stood still while pictures were snapped; the mallards in the twin lakes posed patiently even though we had forgotten to bring bread for them; and the reflecting pool at the library offered unique shots for all our camera buffs. On our way to the Athletic and Convocation Center, where the graduation ceremony would take place, there was time to point out the traditional Senior residence hall — Sorin, Washington Hall, where the theater is housed, the Engineering Building, the Law School, and of course, the Notre Dame Stadium, scene of many an exciting football game. One hundred twenty-five years had elapsed since the little French priest, Father Edward F. Sorin, C.S.C., had started his school in the Indiana wilderness!

Now it was time for Anthony to get in line for the academic procession, adding continuity to what Father Sorin had begun.

The mammoth Athletic Convocation Center was ready. Lights were ablaze from its ceiling — up where heaven begins. American flags were flapping, star-studded blue Indiana State flags were waving, flags from the University of Notre Dame were wafting over the heads of thousands of men, women and children who were gathered for the prestigious commencement of the University of Notre Dame, June 1, 1969. The trumpets blew! The graduates of 1969 were summoned to come forth.

The trumpets were then joined by the saxophones, clarinets, flutes, bassoons and trombones, as well as by the cellos, violas, violins and basses. When the drums and cymbals were given the go-ahead by the conductor, the entire A.C.C. resounded in a magnificent triumphal march, executed in grandiose manner by the University of Notre Dame's orchestra.

President Father Hesburgh greeted the graduates and then congratulated their families for the support and encouragement accorded them. He spoke of Father Sorin and the Notre Dame of the past, and he spoke of broad plans that would make Notre Dame a great University of the future. Then he introduced the commencement speaker, Dr. Daniel P. Moynihan, who had been Assistant to President Kennedy for Urban Affairs, whose rich tones embraced the farthest reaches of the building.

Soon, it was time to call the doctoral candidates forward. The litany had begun. Anthony Robert Black was the fourth to be called. He came forward, be-robed in the blue velvet-trimmed doctoral black gown with his mortar-board tipped ever so jauntily over one eye. In evidence on the hood, as it was slipped over his head, was the white of the liberal arts school and the blue and gold of Notre Dame. As the blue-leather, framed sheepskin, written in Latin, was placed in his hands, I looked over two seats to the tiny baby, now a young lady in college, Stephanie, who had called out at her father's Master's graduation — "There goes Daddy in Papap's shoes!" Anthony's father, wasn't there to lend his shiny shoes this time, but I was certain he was enjoying this moment with his only son.

I looked over one more seat to note Rob's reaction. He was now a high-schooler, whose first interest, like his father's, was history. The next seat was fifth-grader Mary Kay, smiling as only Mary Kay could smile, and beside her, third-grader Bernard, who looked as though he was impressed.

For eighteen years the goal had been the Ph.D. Anthony was leaving the platform, the Ph.D. was his! And the — Ph.T., I had almost forgotten, was mine! I could claim it forever. "It is finished!" I thought. "Hallelujah!"

Professor Anthony Black now had his "union card" to his future as an historian; the Cavendish diary on the Irish Parliament 1174-1776 was squared away for the present and the past; and I had the great satisfaction that I had helped Anthony find his proper niche in life and that he, in turn, was now enabled to pass on a heritage and a love of learning to thousands of young people. And I myself could write a book about it all!

"I never saw my mother look so happy," Mary Kay said to the relatives outside the A.C.C. building as the graduates filed out.

It would be two years later, however, when Anthony's Ph.D. and my Ph.T. would be celebrated

properly with a trip to Ireland for the whole
family. Here Stephanie would discover the Abbey
Theatre, Robbie the Book of Kells at Trinity
College, Mary Kay the dancers on St. Stephen's
Green, and Bernard the high teas! For me would be
the special thrill of finding my paternal
grandmother's one-room, dirt-floored, quaint
little cottage in County Antrim, way in Northern
Ireland, by following directions in a tattered old
prayerbook.

And, three years hence, we would buy our very
own white brick and grey stone home situated on
two acres of wooded land with a fresh bubbly creek
all its own.

But, for now, the last guests and neighbors from
the graduation celebration had gone.
Appropriately, the party broke up after the
fireworks display provided by Prometheus himself,
Anthony.

It was all over. Everyone, save Anthony and
myself, were asleep. As I stood facing the
bathroom mirror brushing my hair, Anthony entered
the room and stood facing the mirror also.

"I thought," he said to his and my image in the
mirror, "that getting the Ph.D. would be my one
and only goal in life. But, now I find I have
another one."

"Oh?" I stopped brushing . . . . and breathing.

"Yes, someday, I want to go to Northern England
and walk on the wall there," he said eagerly.

"The wall? What wall?" I said as I put the brush
down.

"Hadrian's Wall, the Roman Emperor's wall that
was built in 122 A.D. to protect Britain from the

Picts and Scots. There's about one hundred and twenty-five miles of it left. And, I've always had an urge to trace it — to walk on it. To walk on Hadrian's wall — that is my new goal!"

"Glory be," I thought. "Some men have a problem with booze or women or both, but Anthony, he just wants to go walk on a wall."

Then I heard myself say: "Well, if you want to go walk on Hadrian's Wall, you just go walk on it." It was perfectly logical.

"It's not the Great Wall of China," I said to myself, as I fastened a stray end of hair. "This goal could not possibly take eighteen years!"

Ever think of how nice it would be to see a picture of the writers of your favorite hymns and to read about their lives?

If so, you'll love *One Hundred & One Famous Hymns.* Never before has the rich history of our hymn singing traditions been told through the story of our beloved music and its writers.

Chas. Hallberg, Publisher

One Hundred & One Famous Hymns, is truly a magnificent book. It is not only a great contribution to the knowledge of great Christian hymns but is also a notable Christian witness. It is a beautiful work.... I shall do whatever I can to call attention of people to this fine book.

Dr. Norman Vincent Peale

Lovers of music, whether religious or secular, should fine *One Hundred & One Famous Hymns* indispensable to a complete library in church history and music.

The Muncie Star

In assembling his collection, which is a must for every collector of Americana, Johnson not only reprints the most familiar hymn tunes, but tells us how they came about.... By arranging these hymns in historical order, Johnson has developed a history of Christian hymns.... It is a professional job. There will be little dispute on his choice of hymns.

Sunday Press, Atlantic City, N.Y.

Every church library should include this remarkable and much needed book.

The Tulsa World

One Hundred & One Famous Hymns is a big, beautiful book that every Christian will want to own.... The book is a delight to read as well as offering the words and music of our favorite hymns.... It contains interesting information about the people who wrote them and exciting details about the hymns.... There is much more, all equally fascinating and informative.

The Press Gazette, Green Bay, WI